Learning *through* *Assessment*

A Resource Guide for Higher Education

A Publication of the AAHE Assessment Forum

Lion F. Gardiner, Caitlin Anderson, and Barbara L. Cambridge, Editors

This publication should be cited as follows:

AAHE Assessment Forum. (1997). *Learning Through Assessment: A Resource Guide for Higher Education.* Edited by Lion F. Gardiner, Caitlin Anderson, and Barbara L. Cambridge. Washington, DC: American Association for Higher Education.

Any opinions expressed in this publication are those of the editors and other contributors and do not necessarily represent those of the American Association for Higher Education or its members.

For more information about the AAHE Assessment Forum, see *http://www.aahe.org*. Additional copies of this publication are available from AAHE Publications. For ordering information, contact:

American Association for Higher Education
One Dupont Circle, Suite 360
Washington, DC 20036-1110
ph. (202) 293-6440, x11
fax (202) 293-0073
e-mail: *assess@aahe.org*
http://www.aahe.org

ISBN 1-56377-004-0

Table of Contents

Learning Through Assessment:
A RESOURCE GUIDE FOR HIGHER EDUCATION

Acknowledgments

The editors wish to thank the many people who contributed to the publication of this book.

Thomas A. Angelo, who identified the need for a comprehensive resource book and served as external reviewer of this book

Jill Bogard and Cynthia Powell, who located and obtained materials at the American Council of Education library and provided advice to the project

Natalie Borisovets, Carolyn Foote, Dorothy J. Grauer, and Theresa Pugh of the John Cotton Dana Library of Rutgers University, who obtained publications for review

Millie Domenech, who, as project assistant for the AAHE Assessment Forum, assisted with acquisition of materials and locating contact information

Adrianna Kezar, who, as associate director of the ERIC Clearinghouse on Higher Education, provided support and technical assistance with the ERIC database

Bry Pollack, who, as AAHE publications director, helped with editing and publishing decisions

Rutgers University, which provided salary for Lion F. Gardiner during his work on this book

Tracy Tyree, who, as doctoral intern from the University of Maryland-College Park, contributed knowledge about student affairs to several sections of the book and completed editorial work

Pat Wood, who at the ERIC Clearinghouse on Higher Education provided searches of the ERIC database

Several sections of the book are linked with previous work.

Lion F. Gardiner based parts of the Assessment Library on his annotated bibliography and guide, *Assessment Research, Evaluation, and Grading in Higher Education: Overview and Selected Resources* (1992).

Jane Lambert and Mark Connolly shared a draft of an *Assessment Update* article and helped in the conceptualization of the Internet section.

Michael K. Smith and Jama L. Bradley granted AAHE permission to use and update an Assessment Instruments appendix that had appeared in their *Assessment 101 Workbook.*

Many people submitted suggestions and materials to be considered for inclusion in *Learning Through Assessment:*

Mary Kay Alberti, F. King Alexander, James and Susan Anker, Trudy W. Banta, Neil Bernstein, Betty Boatwright, Lois Bollman, Aurora Burke, Madan Capoor, Allen S. Cohen, Mark Connolly, Cynthia Davenport, Linda Denney, Nancy A. Diamond, Steve Ehrmann, Eliot S. Elfner, Peter T. Ewell, Raymond Fischer, Denise Gardner, Steve Gilbert, Judy Diane Grace, Peter J. Gray, Ellen Hay, Frank Jewett, Jane Lambert, David Lutz, Gary Malaney, Ginger M. Marine, Patrick Mayers, Laurie McCown, Jane McGraw, Jo McKenzie, Onie McKenzie, Anne McNeill, Judith E. Miller, Deborah Morris, Jim Morrison, John A. Muffo, Pat Murphy, Larry Nelson, James O. Nichols, Carol Owen, Jacqueline Palmer, Tim Parshall, Nancy Perrin, Douglas B. Reeves, Gloria Rogers, Brit Rönnbäck, Larry Rudner, Ephraim Schechter, Jo Ann Schmitz, Sally Sharp, Michael K. Smith, John Tarnai, Marge Tebo-Messina, Alec Testa, Carol Traxler, George Turner, Theodore C. Wagenaar, and Donald J. Wulff.

Foreword

MARGARET A. MILLER
President, AAHE

More than a decade ago, in 1986, my first assignment at the State Council for Higher Education for Virginia was to write the guidelines for the statewide campus-based assessment program that the General Assembly had just mandated, the first such program in the nation. That same year, the American Association for Higher Education (AAHE) began the Assessment Forum. I think that I am typical of assessment policymakers and practitioners in looking to AAHE ever since for moral and practical support in implementing a program that has profoundly changed the culture of colleges and universities around the country. The association has provided a tent under which people have gathered to discuss how to use assessment both to improve programs and to be more purposeful about what we do for students. In doing so, AAHE has shaped both the assessment movement in this country and the international conversation about higher education's results.

The Assessment Forum builds on that tradition here by bringing together resources useful to all who are laboring in the assessment vineyards. After a decade, an enormous amount of scholarly and pragmatic material on assessment has accumulated. Having sorted and sifted that material, editors Lion Gardiner, Caitlin Anderson, and Barbara Cambridge provide an annotated directory of useful books and articles, journals, newsletters, audiocassettes, organizations, conferences, and electronic resources. Whether you are just getting started in assessment or you have been an assessment practitioner for years, this volume will point you to print resources, conferences, organizations, and sites that can best help you with your work.

Introduction

Learning About Assessment

B A R B A R A L. C A M B R I D G E
Director, AAHE Assessment Forum

Whether you are a new member of a campus assessment committee or an experienced institutional researcher, a faculty member curious about ways your students learn or an administrator responsible for progress toward state performance indicators, a student affairs professional examining practices that contribute to student learning or a student of higher education adding assessment to your knowledge base, this book will provide resources for your learning. The range of resources from audiotapes to books and conferences to websites offers firm theoretical and practical bases for your thinking and practice.

We all learn in different ways. Some people prefer studying a topic minutely before acting, whereas others plunge into practice, through choice or necessity, and analyze, reflect, and theorize later. One beauty of this volume is that you can explore the horizon of multiple resources or begin in your backyard with an example or two. You can choose an auditory way of learning through tapes or a visual one through books and articles. If you like to venture forth on the Internet, you can reach distant shores through websites linked to yet more web sites.

As we began to locate resources to include in this volume, I became curious about ways that past directors of the AAHE Assessment Forum had learned the field. What sources of information and know-how meant the most to them as they continued to learn about assessment during their tenures at AAHE? The past four directors of the Assessment Forum came from different kinds of institutions where they had taught English, German, psychology, and higher education. They came directly from college campuses: Their experience at AAHE put them in touch with people on other campuses who supplied them with further knowledge about assessment.

These directors are each now back in a campus setting, using assessment to help students learn and institutions to improve. Pat Hutchings, although still full-time director of the AAHE Teaching Initiative, is now at the University of Wyoming; Barbara Wright teaches at the University of Connecticut; and Karl Schilling and Tom Angelo teach and have administrative responsibilities at Miami University in Ohio and the University of Miami in Florida, respectively. Like you and me, however, assessment is a part of their larger commitment to teaching and learning. They continue to situate assessment within their main objective of nourishing student learning and continue to seek resources that help them toward this objective.

I asked each assessment director about the five or so resources that contributed most to their knowledge about assessment during their tenure at AAHE. Curious whether some quintessential sources would emerge, I was intrigued to realize that each director had learned in a different way, sometimes from the same sources but often from a consistent perspective revealed in her or his list of important influences. The four perspectives that emerged are learning from practice, learning from and about faculty, learning from and about students, and learning from researchers. To those I add a fifth, my own perspective of learning from expanding contexts. Although the perspectives overlap, and no one person learned in a single way, these five kinds of learning offer different ways of entering the conversation about assessment.

Learning From Practice

The best ways to alienate or intimidate some newcomers to assessment are to refer to complex, large-scale studies; employ jargon such as validity, reliability, and chi squares; and flaunt empirical data. On the other hand, positive ways to encourage persons new to assessment are to offer practical experiences, provide examples, and refer people to their own goals and objectives.

When Barbara Wright identified four written sources of information that meant the most to her, she concluded, "None of this sounds very learned, does it?" She was referring not to the quality of the referenced materials but to her reliance on materials that emerged from practice and that were presented in nontechnical terms.

First, Barbara remembered a collection of assessment instruments from MindaRae Amiran at SUNY College at Fredonia, materials marked by their "openendedness, their focus on very simple but profound educational questions, and the creativity that went into their design." These materials opened up for Barbara "a whole different way of thinking about knowledge and assessment that was much more congenial and authentic than the multiple-choice test with its almost inevitable triviality and lack of room for individual student expressions."

Concrete examples were also important to Barbara. In referring to Cliff Adelman's *Performance and Judgment: Essays on Principles and Practice in the Assessment of College Student Learning*, also cited by Tom Angelo, Barbara lauded the book for its useful examples. She advised, "Concrete examples tend to be vastly underestimated by the initiated, but for people coming to assessment from other academic disciplines besides education, they're absolutely essential." She applauded the book's directness, lack of jargon, and suggestions for ways to customize assessment to local needs.

That customizing was central in another book Barbara recommended, a 1954 (yes, '54) book on general education. Paul Dressel and Lewis Mayhew's *General Education: Explorations in Evaluation* reports on a government-funded study of general education focused on how to be effective with a generation of nontraditional college-goers. According to Barbara, it "contains nice examples of statements of goals and objectives for things like critical thinking in science or aesthetic response to art and literature." Its "clear and unpretentious style" makes it a book to which Barbara returns. She remains "tickled to no end that the things we're busy huffing and puffing about today were being treated so carefully and well forty years ago."

Although some issues may be the same, their treatment is often different in today's environment for higher education. Barbara finds Trudy Banta's *Making a Difference,* a central resource also for Tom, a current source of examples of ways that faculty, departments, campuses, and states are using assessment to improve programs, services, and student learning. Current practices in multiple sites offer ideas for adoption and adaptation at other sites.

Learning from practice offers one perspective on assessment. Barbara Wright's choices of resources emphasize the efficacy of examples, plain talk, and attention to practical goals and methods.

Learning From and About Faculty

Pat Hutchings also emphasized starting on the issue of assessment "close to the classroom." She writes that "the idea that assessment needs to be faculty-driven and embedded in the classroom practice is now gospel, but a decade ago it was by no means so." She credits *Classroom Assessment Techniques: A Handbook for Faculty* by K. Patricia Cross and Thomas A. Angelo with helping to promote today's view. According to Pat, the book identifies "faculty as active agents of improvement through inquiry into the dynamics of teaching and learning in their own practice."

Recognizing the intimidation factor of assessment, Pat advocates the book's "bite-sized, doable strategies that we mere-mortal faculty, unschooled in the methods of educational research, can actually imagine using in our own practice. Assessment need not be a high-tech activity of specialists but something that 'regular faculty' can engage in. Gathering information from our own students about their learning is not only useful but intellectually interesting."

This emphasis on the intellectual aspect of assessment is central in Pat's second choice of reading material. *Involvement in Learning: Realizing the Potential of American Higher Education,* published by the Study Group on the Conditions of Excellence in American Higher Education of the National Institute of Education, is a national report on educational reform, not, as Pat says, "typically the kind of thing you want to curl up by the fire with." Yet, Pat credits this report with "putting assessment on the map as an educational issue." Although many people in higher education viewed assessment as external in origin, this report established the educational foundations for assessment, its potential for improving learning. It was this report, not external mandates, that led AAHE to sponsor its first national conference on assessment in October 1985.

Pat's emphasis on the intellectual and educational aspects of assessment central to faculty continues in her choice of Donald Schön's *The Reflective Practitioner: How Professionals Think in Action* as an important book in her thinking. She notes that this book is not about assessment as readers of this volume probably think of it, but it deals with periodic data gathering, which Schön sees as an important aspect of professional practice — a habit of self-examination undertaken in a spirit of both intellectual and ethical responsibility for understanding and improving the consequences of our actions as professionals.

Pat walks this talk. As director of AAHE's Teaching Initiative, she works with faculty in improving their "teaching and learning not by promoting any particular pedagogy but by helping campuses develop the conditions in which faculty can be more professional and scholarly about their approach to teaching."

Another way to approach assessment, then, is through the lens of intellectual and ethical responsibility. Faculty who engage in assessment are acting professionally and responsibly toward their intellectual and educational enterprise.

Learning From and About Students

That enterprise, of course, is chiefly about students. Karl Schilling's choices emphasize the centrality of students in all assessment practices. He recommends books about student development, the cultures in which students move, and assessment methods that yield insights into student life and learning.

According to Karl, Michael Moffatt's *Coming of Age in New Jersey,* Paul F. Kluge's *Alma Mater,* and Douglas Heath's *Growing Up in College* all "provide examples of observational studies of student development. The narratives the three authors provide are strong examples of the power of the story to convey 'assessment' in a persuasive way." In addition, Karl mentions Donna Killian Duffy and Janet Wright Jones' *Teaching Within the Rhythms of the Semester* as a reliable source for developing a "sense of appropriate timing" in students' lives "in order to create effective interventions and program offerings." The authors "connect cognitive development theory to the course syllabi, focusing on how students at various stages of development understand syllabi" and progress in their learning.

Although student development is important, the cultures in which students operate significantly influence their learning. Karl recommends Neil Howe and Bill Strauss's *13th Gen: Abort, Retry, Ignore, Fail?* because it "focuses on the need to look more broadly at the cultural factors that influence a generation of college students. Any attempt to assess institutional impact needs to be very cognizant of the context in which the students exist."

Three publications advocate approaches to assessment that match objectives of the assessment. According to Karl, Caryn McTigue Musil's *Students at the Center: Feminist Assessment* strongly "advocates for qualitative approaches to assessment" that will "support the development of conversations rather than defensiveness and meaninglessness that frequently come from more normative approaches." Both Pat Hutchings' *Behind Outcomes* and Maryann Jacobi, Alexander Astin, and Frank Ayala Jr.'s *College Student*

Outcomes Assessment: A Talent Development Perspective move beyond the value-added model of assessment to provide insights about what makes a difference in quality educational experiences for students. Tom Angelo added about the latter book: "Talent development is a radical and potentially liberating metaphor for assessment."

To ensure quality educational experiences, institutional organization must be sound. Karl recommends W. Edwards Deming's *The New Economics for Industry, Government, and Education* for the idea of "profound knowledge," the kind of information that is useful in helping institutions learn to see how to make systems more effective. The kind of "descriptive account" Deming finds valuable in prompting change leads to insights about areas that need improvement for the benefit of all stakeholders, including students.

Karl Schilling's current FIPSE-supported multi-institutional study of how students use their time is a natural extension of his focus on learning about and from students as a basis for creating pedagogical and assessment strategies. Viewing learning through the eyes of students enables choices of assessment measures that more accurately contribute to students' learning.

Learning From Researchers

Researchers are more advanced learners: They have spent the intellectual energy, time, and resources to study and add to knowledge about a particular area. Tom Angelo identifies his "faculty in assessment," people who have influenced him even more than books. On his list are Alexander Astin, Trudy Banta, Pat Cross, Peter Ewell, Don Farmer, Pat Hutchings, Richard Light, Ted Marchese, Marcia Mentkowski, Karl Schilling, Ralph Wolff, and Barbara Wright. He notes that "it would be a mistake to underestimate the importance of personal contacts and communications in the genesis of the assessment movement."

Even as Tom lists publications that have influenced his thinking, he accentuates the authors. Seven books by important authors have guided Tom's thinking about and work with assessment. The most influential book that he has read on higher education, one that "changed forever" his ideas about thinking, writing, teaching, and assessing, is Mina Shaughnessy's *Errors and Expectations: A Guide for the Teacher of Basic Writing.* Shaughnessy took a deep approach to analysis of what might seem like intractable student mistakes. Tom was inspired by her approach to find from students the reasons for their responses. He writes, "Even before I knew the term 'assessment,' Shaughnessy's book and the work of other writing teachers/researchers such as Anne Berthoff, Peter Elbow, Toby Fulwiler, Dixie Goswami, and Elaine Maimon set me on a course that led me to Classroom Assessment."

In mentioning *Performance and Judgment,* a book also central to Barbara Wright's thinking, Tom says of the editor: "Cliff Adelman played a key role in launching and shaping the assessment movement, and this volume is now historical evidence of his vision and early influence. Many of the essays raise questions and offer caveats that are still valid." Adelman established, in Tom's view, that "assessment is more a question of political will than technical skill."

Although political will is central, technical skill is essential, too. Tom states that through conversations and presentations as well as edited books, Trudy Banta has influenced his thinking. Her two books *Making a Difference: Outcomes of a Decade of Assessment in Higher Education* and *Assessment in Practice: Putting Principles to Work on College Campuses* provide a "great crash course in assessment" by providing "the best and most comprehensive sources of examples of assessment practices."

Tom goes on to identify Peter Ewell as "the most knowledgeable, thoughtful, and influential writer and speaker on assessment." Tom states that "no one has helped me more in understanding the policy implications of assessment and in seeing their practical implications for institutions. If I had to recommend only one of his many excellent pieces, it would be 'To Capture the Ineffable: New Forms of Assessment in Higher Education.'"

The work of five other expert authors receives Tom's accolades. Of Richard Light, Judith B. Singer, and John B. Willett's *By Design: Planning Research on Higher Education,* Tom says, "This book explains how to design useful research for assessment and improvement purposes. My favorite quote is 'You can't fix by analysis what you bungled by design.'" Of Ernest Pascarella and Patrick Terenzini's *How College Affects Students: Findings and Insights from Twenty Years of Research,* Tom states, "This is the best and only one-volume review of the literature on the effects of college. In my self-education, it provided the research frame for my thinking about the desirable and the possible in higher education outcomes."

A fourth way to learn about assessment, then, is turning to researchers, those learners whose analysis and reflection have added new knowledge to the field and who have published pieces that benefit inexperienced and experienced assessment practitioners and researchers.

Learning From Expanding Contexts

Each advance in my own thinking about assessment has come through operating in an expanded context. What I have read, written, and practiced in assessment has been tested by its application in a wider context.

"Using Portfolios at Indiana University," a 1988 publication, helped me realize that my classroom assessment practice could fit into an institution's practice. After experience with using portfolios in my individual classes and then in a campus's large writing program, I began working with colleagues across disciplines and campuses in a plan for all of Indiana University. The resulting document looked at rationale, history, issues, relationship to institutional mission, and proposed practices, contending that "the university must find a method to track and to measure the total writing experiences of each student in order to monitor and improve its educational product." Although the proposed plan was adopted in limited rather than comprehensive ways, I learned to think institutionally from this assessment planning across a set of campuses.

Experience with the second edition of a book Pat mentioned also pushed my thinking beyond my own classroom. Thomas A. Angelo and K. Patricia Cross's *Classroom Assessment Techniques: A Handbook for College Teachers* broadened my repertoire of ways to learn continuously about how students were learning but also enabled discussion with faculty from many disciplines about our pedagogies. After colleagues and I tested and examined results of using multiple techniques, we applied analyses of our classroom assessment practices in both formative and summative situations, learning in the process how to talk with one another about our teaching. We learned to make our teaching public through helping our students make their learning processes open and changeable.

Another kind of contextualization came after I read Musil's *Students at the Center*, which Karl also identified as significant to his thinking. My ah-ha moment came when I realized what the book contends: "What people measure is—and ought to be—what they value, and the way people measure it also is a choice grounded in values." I extended my belief that pedagogy embodies values to a belief that assessment embodies values. This book identifies feminist assessment as student-centered, participatory, affected by context and culture, decentered, and evoking action. It is a "process more concerned with improvement than testing, with nurturing progression than with final judgment." This book propelled me to explain my assessment practices theoretically at two national conferences, CCCC and AAHE, so that my context for learning widened yet again.

The next context for assessment that has expanded my thinking is accreditation. The NCA/CIHE *Assessment Handbook* taught me that my own assessment practices have something to do with the evaluation of my institution. I learned about the North Central Association's characteristics of a good assessment program: It "flows from the institution's mission, has a conceptual framework, has faculty ownership/responsibility, has institution-wide support, uses multiple measures, provides feedback to students and the institution, is cost-effective, does not restrict access, equity or diversity, leads to improvement, and has a process for evaluating the assessment plan." New to systemic thinking, I was excited that the marks of what I knew to be effective assessment in the classroom and curriculum could guide the university as a whole.

Lastly, the discovery of *The Student Learning Imperative,* a publication of the American College Personnel Association, awoke me to the similar aims of student affairs professionals and faculty members. Because both are dedicated to student learning, they need to work collaboratively to assess their progress toward that end.

Learning through expanding contexts brought me to AAHE. I now learn from three new sources: AAHE members from many colleges and universities, organizations with whom AAHE collaborates, and experienced AAHE staff. AAHE is fortunate to have as one of its vice presidents a leading expert on learning and assessment, Ted Marchese, and as its president Margaret Miller, a leader experienced on the campus and on the state level in matters of assessment and accountability.

You, too, can learn from the AAHE context. Just as past directors have offered their modes of learning, this book provides you with many resources for your own expanded learning. We welcome your participation in the continual goal of locating resources by soliciting your responses to the present contents and your suggestions of additional resources that are central to your thinking and practice. We hope that this book becomes a starting point for your own widening context of learning about and through assessment.

Works Cited

Adelman, Clifford. (Ed.). (1987). *Performance and judgment: Essays on principles and practice in the assessment of college student learning.* Washington, DC: US Department of Education, Office of Research.

Amiran, MindaRae. (1988). *Campus assessment materials.* Fredonia, NY: State University of New York College at Fredonia.

Angelo, Thomas A., & Cross, K. Patricia. (1993). *Classroom assessment techniques: A handbook for college teachers* (2nd ed.). San Francisco: Jossey-Bass.

Banta, Trudy W., Lund, Jon, Black, Karen, & Oblander, Frances. (1995). *Assessment in practice: Putting principles to work on college campuses.* San Francisco: Jossey-Bass.

Banta, Trudy W., & Associates. (1993). *Making a difference: Outcomes of a decade of assessment in higher education.* San Francisco: Jossey-Bass.

Commission on Institutions of Higher Education. (1991). *Assessment workbook.* Chicago: North Central Association of Colleges and Schools.

Cross, K. Patricia, & Angelo, Thomas A. (1988). *Classroom assessment techniques: A handbook for faculty.* Ann Arbor, MI: University of Michigan, National Center for Research to Improve Postsecondary Teaching and Learning.

Deming, W. Edwards. (1993). *The new economics for industry, government, and education.* Cambridge, MA: Massachusetts Institute of Technology, Center for Advanced Engineering Study.

Dressel, Peter & Mayhew, Lewis. (1954). *General education: Explorations in evaluation.* Washington, DC: American Council on Education.

Duffy, Donna Killian, & Jones, Janet Wright. (1995). *Teaching within the rhythms of the semester.* San Francisco: Jossey-Bass.

Ewell, Peter. (1991). To capture the ineffable: New forms of assessment in higher education. In *Reprise 1991.* Washington, DC: American Association for Higher Education.

Heath, Douglas. (1968). *Growing up in college.* San Francisco: Jossey-Bass.

Howe, Neil, & Strauss, Bill. (1993). *13th Gen: Abort, retry, ignore, fail?* New York: Vintage Books.

Hutchings, Pat. (1989). *Behind outcomes: Contexts and questions for assessment.* Washington, DC: American Association for Higher Education.

Intercampus Committee on Writing and Assessment of Writing. (1988). *Using Portfolios at Indiana University.* Indianapolis, IN: IUPUI.

Jacobi, Maryann, Astin, Alexander, & Ayala, Frank, Jr. (1987). *College student outcomes assessment: A talent development perspective* (ASHE-ERIC Higher Education Report No. 7). Washington, DC: Association for the Study of Higher Education.

Kluge, Paul F. (1993). *Alma mater: A college homecoming.* Reading, MA: Addison-Wesley.

Light, Richard, Singer, Judith D., & Willett, John B. (1990). *By design: Planning research for higher education.* Cambridge, MA: Harvard University.

Moffatt, Michael. (1989). *Coming of age in New Jersey: College and American culture.* New Brunswick, NJ: Rutgers University Press.

Musil, Caryn McTigue. (Ed.). (1992). *Students at the center: Feminist assessment*. Washington, DC: Association of American Colleges.

Pascarella, Ernest, & Terenzini, Patrick T. (1991). *How college affects students: Findings and insights from twenty years of research*. San Francisco: Jossey-Bass.

Schön, Donald A. (1983). *The reflective practitioner: How professionals think in action*. New York: Basic Books.

Schroeder, Charles; Astin, Alexander; Astin, Helen; Bloland, Paul; Cross, K. Patricia; Hurst, James; Kuh, George; Marchese, Ted; Nuss, Elizabeth; Pascarella, Ernest; Pruitt, Anne; & Rooney, Michael. (1994). *The student learning imperative: Implications for student affairs*. Washington, DC: American College Personnel Association.

Shaughnessy, Mina. (1977). *Errors and expectations: A guide for the teacher of basic writing*. New York: Oxford University Press.

Study Group on the Conditions of Excellence in American Higher Education. (1984). *Involvement in learning: Realizing the potential of American higher education*. Washington, DC: National Institute of Education.

Principles of Good Practice for Assessing Student Learning

Developed under the auspices of the AAHE Assessment Forum, December 1992.

1 The assessment of student learning begins with educational values. Assessment is not an end in itself but a vehicle for educational improvement. Its effective practice, then, begins with and enacts a vision of the kinds of learning we most value for students and strive to help them achieve. Educational values should drive not only what we choose to assess but also how we do so. Where questions about educational mission and values are skipped over, assessment threatens to be an exercise in measuring what's easy, rather than a process of improving what we really care about.

2 Assessment is most effective when it reflects an understanding of learning as multidimensional, integrated, and revealed in performance over time. Learning is a complex process. It entails not only what students know but what they can do with what they know; it involves not only knowledge and abilities but values, attitudes, and habits of mind that affect both academic success and performance beyond the classroom. Assessment should reflect these understandings by employing a diverse array of methods, including those that call for actual performance, using them over time so as to reveal change, growth, and increasing degrees of integration. Such an approach aims for a more complete and accurate picture of learning, and therefore firmer bases for improving our students' educational experience.

3 Assessment works best when the programs it seeks to improve have clear, explicitly stated purposes. Assessment is a goal-oriented process. It entails comparing educational performance with educational purposes and expectations — those derived from the institution's mission, from faculty intentions in program and course design, and from knowledge of students' own goals. Where program purposes lack specificity or agreement, assessment as a process pushes a campus toward clarity about where to aim and what standards to apply; assessment also prompts attention to where and how program goals will be taught and learned. Clear, shared, implementable goals are the cornerstone for assessment that is focused and useful.

4 Assessment requires attention to outcomes but also and equally to the experiences that lead to those outcomes. Information about outcomes is of high importance; where students "end up" matters greatly. But to improve outcomes, we need to know about student experience along the way — about the curricula, teaching, and kind of student effort that lead to particular outcomes. Assessment can help us understand which students learn best under what conditions; with such knowledge comes the capacity to improve the whole of their learning.

5 Assessment works best when it is ongoing, not episodic. Assessment is a process whose power is cumulative. Though isolated, "one-shot" assessment can be better than none, improvement is best fostered when assessment entails a linked series of activities undertaken over time. This may mean tracking the process of individual students, or of cohorts of students; it may mean collecting the same examples of student performance or using the same instrument semester after semester. The point is to monitor progress toward intended goals in a spirit of continuous improvement. Along the way, the assessment process itself should be evaluated and refined in light of emerging insights.

6 Assessment fosters wider improvement when representatives from across the educational community are involved. Student learning is a campus-wide responsibility, and assessment is a way of enacting that responsibility. Thus, while assessment efforts may start small, the aim over time is to involve people from across the educational community. Faculty play an especially important role, but assessment's questions can't be fully addressed without participation by student-affairs educators, librarians, administrators, and students. Assessment may also involve individuals from beyond the campus (alumni/ae, trustees, employers) whose experience can enrich the sense of appropriate aims and standards for learning. Thus understood, assessment is not a task for small groups of experts but a collaborative activity; its aim is wider, better-informed attention to student learning by all parties with a stake in its improvement.

7 Assessment makes a difference when it begins with issues of use and illuminates questions that people really care about.
Assessment recognizes the value of information in the process of improvement. But to be useful, information must be connected to issues or questions that people really care about. This implies assessment approaches that produce evidence that relevant parties will find credible, suggestive, and applicable to decisions that need to be made. It means thinking in advance about how the information will be used, and by whom. The point of assessment is not to gather data and return "results"; it is a process that starts with the questions of decision-makers, that involves them in the gathering and interpreting of data, and that informs and helps guide continuous improvement.

8 Assessment is most likely to lead to improvement when it is part of a larger set of conditions that promote change.
Assessment alone changes little. Its greatest contribution comes on campuses where the quality of teaching and learning is visibly valued and worked at. On such campuses, the push to improve educational performance is a visible and primary goal of leadership; improving the quality of undergraduate education is central to the institution's planning, budgeting, and personnel decisions. On such campuses, information about learning outcomes is seen as an integral part of decision making, and avidly sought.

9 Through assessment, educators meet responsibilities to students and to the public. There is a compelling public stake in education. As educators, we have a responsibility to the publics that support or depend on us to provide information about the ways in which our students meet goals and expectations. But that responsibility goes beyond the reporting of such information; our deeper obligation — to ourselves, our students, and society — is to improve. Those to whom educators are accountable have a corresponding obligation to support such attempts at improvement.

Authors: Alexander W. Astin, Trudy W. Banta, K. Patricia Cross, Elaine El-Khawas, Peter T. Ewell, Pat Hutchings, Theodore J. Marchese, Kay M. McClenney, Marcia Mentkowski, Margaret A. Miller, E. Thomas Moran, and Barbara D. Wright

This document was developed under the auspices of the AAHE Assessment Forum with support from the Fund for the Improvement of Postsecondary Education with additional support for publication and dissemination from the Exxon Education Foundation. Copies may be made without restriction. The *Principles of Good Practice for Assessing Student Learning* is also available on the AAHE web site, *http://www.aahe.org.*

Learning Through Assessment Structure

Because of widespread interest in assessment, books, journal articles, institutional reports, and Internet-based resources abound. This book collects in one place some of the most useful of these assessment resources to help campuses begin or expand assessment activities. It is designed to help college and university faculty members, student affairs professionals, and administrators; state higher education agency staff members; and others who want to improve quality in their courses, programs, institutions or higher education systems.

The book is divided into two major sections. The **Assessment Library,** written by Lion F. Gardiner, includes general references, an annotated list of periodicals related to assessment, and a lengthy annotated bibliography to assessment resources. The general references provide a starting point for faculty and others new to assessment, while the annotated bibliography is comprehensively indexed to be of use to practitioners in search of specific references. In this section readers can find references to answer a wide array of questions.

The other section of the book, compiled by Caitlin Anderson, is made up of six distinct parts.

Associations and Organizations

This guide to groups which disseminate information about assessment includes regional accrediting associations, national higher education associations, regional networks, and institutional assessment centers.

Conferences

25 conferences ranging from regional to national and general to discipline specific are included with contact information for each. Special indication is made if the sponsoring group is described in the previous section.

Instruments

This list was originally published by Michael K. Smith and Jama L. Bradley, who granted AAHE permission to reprint it here. The AAHE Assessment Forum updated the contact information so that it is accurate as of April 1997. The list classifies tests according to student status and includes instruments for assessment of critical thinking and writing.

Internet Resources

Because the Internet can be a valuable resource for assessment practitioners, references to institutional World Wide Web sites, assessment related listservs, and other information sites are listed here. A search engine can lead to additional valuable resources. For example, with a list of peer institutions, a search of the pertinent home pages may lead to institutional assessment documents on-line.

Multimedia Resources

Videotapes of interest to assessment practitioners are described here. In addition, the annual AAHE Assessment & Quality Conference, with the assistance of Mobiltape, Inc., offers audiotapes of selected conference sessions. Listed are the best selling tapes from the 1994, 1995, and 1996 conferences.

Technology

Included in this section are references to institutional projects, websites, and articles which address issues of technology and assessment.

Also included for your information is a **Glossary** of terms used frequently in assessment. The book concludes with two indexes: an **Author Index** of those whose works are abstracted in the References section and a **Keyword Index** to the entire Resource Guide.

Readers can help the AAHE Assessment Forum expand and improve future editions of *Learning Through Assessment.* Please call (202-293-6440), fax (202-293-0073), write, or e-mail any suggestions you have for additional resources or sections to this guide. Send examples of institutional documents that might be of interest to other assessment practitioners. The AAHE Assessment Forum addresses are AAHE, One Dupont Circle, Suite 360, Washington, DC 20036, or e-mail: *assess@aahe.org.*

Assessment Library

The resources in this section are some of the best known and most useful for both novices and more experienced assessment practitioners. They include books, periodicals, journal articles, reports by government agencies and higher education associations, and reports of research and of assessment experiences on individual campuses. The coverage of the resources reflects the nature of the assessment literature now available.

A key to the wise use of assessment and evaluation for improving institutional effectiveness is to understand the systemic interrelationships among all institutional components and functions. For example, the efficacy of curricula depends on the quality of instruction in courses, and the effectiveness of both curricula and instruction depend, in turn, on the quality of academic advising and campus psychological climate and the degree to which the organizational culture values human development and supports high standards of performance for everyone.

Likewise, outcome, input, and process goals and objectives and their assessment and evaluation are all naturally connected to one another. Each one plays a critical role in understanding the organization—a college or university, its programs, and its courses—as a unified, coherent *system,* including its various clients and constituents. Tinkering with assessment at the fringes of the institutional enterprise may not produce much useful information or lead to significant improvement in quality because other, unconsidered but important variables, factors, or forces interact to obscure relationships or maintain the status quo.

In practice, however, input assessment is often scanty and, although institutional outcomes are produced by processes, outcome assessment is by no means always connected to process assessment such that institutional performance and quality can be systematically improved. Assessment and evaluation may not be connected to carefully defined educational outcome goals and objectives or may not be used at all. *Assessment is useful only if its results are used to improve the quality of an institution's, program's, or course's outcomes.*

The resources in this assessment library, and the book as a whole, have been selected to reflect this systemic, integrated approach to thinking about institutions, programs, and courses. This diverse array of resources can help practitioners understand and improve the various complex structural and functional components of their institutions and their interrelationships.

PERIODICALS

A number of periodicals are devoted to assessment and evaluation in education generally or in higher education specifically; thirteen of these are described here. Each one is briefly described, together with information about its publisher, generally a professional association or commercial firm. A number of the journals are devoted to evaluation theory and practice and may have articles of value dealing with the more technical aspects of assessment and evaluation in higher education.

The list does not include journals that specialize in evaluation in specific disciplines other than education. Many education journals contain occasional articles or special issues on assessment. Some of these appear among the references in the next section. Notable developments related to assessment are often reported in *The Chronicle of Higher Education, AAHE Bulletin,* and *Change* magazine, as well as in *Assessment Update.*

Most publishers now maintain a presence on the World Wide Web. The Web contains information about some periodicals, and sometimes the contents of current or previous issues are available in archives for reading and downloading. Some of these Web sites also contain, or are linked to, other useful information related to assessment.

Adult Assessment Forum
P. O. Box 52069
Phoenix, Arizona 85072-9381
ph. (602) 894-5559
fax (602) 894-8885
http://www.intered.com/forum1.htm

This quarterly journal specializes in the theory and application of outcome assessment and quality improvement in institutions focusing on the education of adults. Contents include editorials by authorities in assessment, new applications of Continuous Quality Improvement in higher education, and reports from assessment programs in colleges and universities.

Applied Measurement in Education
Oscar and Luella Buros Center for Testing
135 Bancroft Hall
University of Nebraska-Lincoln
Lincoln, NE 68588-0348
http://www.unl.edu/buros

This journal publishes articles that apply research on measurement to educational processes, including reviews of tests.

Assessment and Evaluation in Higher Education
Carfax Publishing Company
875-81 Massachusetts Avenue
Cambridge, MA 02139
ph. (617) 354-1425
fax (617) 354-6875
http://www.carfax.co.uk/aeh-ad.htm

This international journal contains articles concerning all aspects of assessment and evaluation in higher education, particularly research and reports that can help increase student learning and faculty, instructional, and institutional development.

Assessment Update: Progress, Trends, and Practices in Higher Education.
Jossey-Bass, Inc., Publishers
350 Sansome Street
San Francisco, CA 94104-1310
ph. (800) 956-7739
or (415) 433-1740
fax (800) 605-2665
http://www.josseybass.com

This bimonthly newsletter publishes articles, conference announcements, book reviews, and other items relevant to assessment in higher education.

Educational and Psychological Measurement
Sage Publications, Inc.
2455 Teller Road
Thousand Oaks, CA 91320
ph. (805) 499-0721
fax (805) 499-0871
e-mail: info@sagepub.com
http://www.sagepub.com/sagepage/welcome.html

This journal, published six times each year, includes articles dealing with the measurement of individual differences in education, industry, and government; problems,

development and use of tests; descriptions of testing programs; and other topics relevant to tests.

Educational Assessment
Lawrence Erlbaum Associates, Inc.
10 Industrial Ave.
Mahwah, NJ 07430-2262
ph. (201) 236-9500
fax (201) 236-0072
http://www.erlbaum.com/989.htm

This general journal reports research on all aspects, both theoretical and applied, of assessing individuals, groups, and educational programs at all levels and in all environments.

Educational Evaluation and Policy Analysis
American Educational Research Association
1230 17th Street, NW
Washington, DC 20036-3078
ph. (202) 223-9486
fax (202) 775-1824
e-mail: aera@aera.net
http://aera.net/pubs/eepa/index.html

This journal, published quarterly, contains articles related to evaluation in education and analysis of education policy.

Evaluation and Program Planning
Elsevier Science
Box 945
New York, NY 10159-0945
ph. (212) 633-3730
fax (212) 633-3680
e-mail: usinfo-f@elsevier.com
http://www.elsevier.nl

This international journal is for evaluators and planners in various sectors, including education.

Journal of Educational Measurement
National Council on Measurement in Education
1230 17th Street, NW
Washington, DC 20036-3078
ph. (202) 223-9318
fax (202) 775-1824
http://ncme.iupui.edu/ncme/ncme.html

This quarterly journal contains research, reports, reviews, and comments on previous articles published in the journal, on topics related to educational measurement.

New Directions for Institutional Research
Jossey-Bass, Inc., Publishers
350 Sansome Street
San Francisco, CA 94104-1310
ph. (800) 956-7739
or (415) 433-1740
fax (800) 605-2665
http://www.josseybass.com

This quarterly, paperback book series contains articles by experts and practitioners on various aspects of assessment and evaluation in higher education.

Planning for Higher Education
Society for College and University Planning (SCUP)
4251 Plymouth Road, Suite D
Ann Arbor, MI 48105-2785
ph. (313) 998-7832
fax (313) 998-6532
e-mail: *jolene@scup.ra.itd.umich.edu*
http://www.umich.edu/~scup/PHE.html

This quarterly journal of the Society for College and University Planning publishes articles related to academic, administrative, financial, and facilities planning, including research of value to educational decision making.

Research in Higher Education
Human Sciences Press
233 Spring Street
New York, NY 10013-1578
ph. (212) 807-1047

The journal of the Association for Institutional Research (AIR) reports empirical studies related to students, faculty, and administrators that are oriented toward improving institutional effectiveness, as well as brief notes on methods.

Studies in Educational Evaluation
Center for the Study of Evaluation
Graduate School of Education and Information
120 Moore Hall, Mail Box 951522
UCLA
Los Angeles, CA 90095
ph. (310) 206-1532
fax (310) 825-3883
e-mail: *cse@ucla.edu*
http://www.cse.ucla.edu

This publication reports research on all aspects of evaluation in education.

REFERENCES

The publications described in this section represent only a fraction of the now-rich and growing literature on assessment in higher education. They have been selected because of their general usefulness, review and synthesis of widely scattered research, attention to topics of specialized interest, or description of novel approaches to issues or problems. They are all relatively easily available through libraries or from their publishers or the ERIC Document Reproduction Service. Together, they encompass most of the topics, issues, and situations that concern assessment practitioners today.

Most of these references have been published since 1985. Others, although published before this date, are of enduring value or of historical significance in the development of assessment in higher education.

This section, and the entire book, strive to be inclusive of various aspects of institutions of higher education. One result of this effort has been to include references of special interest to student affairs professionals. Thanks to the work of Tracy Tyree, a doctoral student in college student personnel at the University of Maryland and an intern with the AAHE Assessment Forum, there are publications throughout this section that focus on the assessment of learning outside the classroom.

The ERIC data base contains numerous institutional and state plans and reports and conference presentations not included here, many of which are of significant value. They can be easily identified in the ERIC data base by using specific keyword combinations. (For information about the ERIC system and how to use its data base of education resources, see the Higher Education Research Centers section in both the Association and Organizations and the Internet Resources chapters.)

All of the references in this section have been annotated with publications in hand except for those whose abstracts are followed by "(ERIC)." These annotations were developed from information in the ERIC data base.

Most resources contain information relevant to more than one topic. The specific nature of a book, article, or report can be determined from its title, its abstract, and the keyword symbols that appear immediately after the abstract.

References of General Interest

A number of references are of sufficiently general interest to mention them here. These are often excellent places to start when beginning to think about an issue or for people new to assessment.

Student development and college effects on students. Considerable empirical research has accumulated on student development in college, some of it of great importance to teachers and managers of the educational process and specifically to people involved with assessment. The books by Astin (1993), Cross and Steadman (1996), Gardiner (1994), and Pascarella and Terenzini (1991) review and synthesize large amounts of research relevant to student development, college effects on students, and institutional functioning, or describe extensive studies of how institutions affect students and provide descriptions of assessment research methodology. These references can help an institution identify specific student outcomes, develop an overarching philosophy and plan for assessment, and suggest specific variables and methodologies it might use.

Mission statements, goals, and objectives. The books by Bloom (1956), Gardiner (1989), Harrow (1972), Krathwohl, Bloom, and Masia (1964), and Lenning (1977) can be of particular assistance in understanding mission statements and the roles and classification of goals and objectives and the importance of and methods for choosing and defining them with great care as a foundation and necessary precondition for assessment and as a means of clearly linking the assessment enterprise to institutional and unit mission statements.

General assessment textbooks. Angelo and Cross (1993), Astin (1991), Erwin (1991), Light, Singer, and Willett (1990), and Nichols (1995a, 1995c) are general textbooks on assessment design and use. They contain resources that can help both novices and more experienced assessment practitioners with both theoretical and practical issues as they design and implement their assessment research and interpret their results.

Test design, measurement, evaluation, and statistical aspects of assessment. Of special technical interest with respect to the more theoretical aspects of assessment, test design, measurement, and evaluation are Anderson, Ball, Murphy, and Associates (1975), Astin (1991, 1993), Bloom, Hastings, and Madaus (1971), Carey (1994), Cronbach (1984), Dressell (1976), Light, Singer, and Willett (1990), Linn (1993), Pascarella and Terenzini (1991), Terenzini (1989), Witkin (1984), and Yancey (1988).

Assessment on campus. A number of compendia of good practice describe, often in the words of local practitioners, plans, programs, and results of assessment activities on various types of campuses around North America. These publications are useful because they can describe conditions similar to those in readers' home institutions and help identify creative methods and potential problems. Among these books are Banta and Associates (1993), Banta, Lund, Black, and Oblander (1996), and Nichols (1996b).

General conceptual framework for assessment and improvement of quality. The Education Criteria for the Malcolm Baldrige National Quality Award (Education Pilot Criteria, 1995) administered by the U. S. National Institute of Standards and

Technology deserves a place here. The Criteria can provide an institution with a framework for systematically thinking about quality on campus and the assessment evidence it requires to understand and improve this quality.

Keywords

Annotated Bibliography

1. AAHE Assessment Forum. (1992). Principles of good practice for assessing student learning. Washington, DC: American Association for Higher Education. 4 pp.

These nine principles articulate and explain a wisdom of practice that has emerged from many years of national experience in assessment in the United States. Authored by 12 experienced assessment professionals in higher education, the Principles provide a concise guide to good practice in assessment. Specific principles address student learning, educational values, the purposes of assessment, the linkage of educational processes to outcomes, frequency of assessment, faculty involvement in assessment, use of results, integration of assessment with other institutional activities, and the public value of assessment. Copies are available from the AAHE Assessment Forum. GN, H, OA, PP, TH, U

2. Abler, Rose M. & Sedlacek, William E. (1986). Nonreactive measures in student affairs research. (Report No. RR-5-86). College Park, MD: University of Maryland, Counseling Center. (ERIC Document Reproduction Service No. ED 278 934). 14pp.

This report focuses on the value of nonreactive methodology in better understanding college students. Nonreactive methodology is defined as "unobtrusive methods of collecting data in which participant reaction to the process of data collection does not interfere with the response" (p. 4). Examples of previous studies using nonreactive approaches are described. Additionally, the authors discuss the advantages and disadvantages of nonreactive techniques and outline steps for doing this type of research. Nonreactive methodology is intended to enhance information on students, not replace other forms of data collection. MT, PR, SN

3. Achieving institutional effectiveness through assessment: A resource manual to support WASC institutions. (1992). Oakland, CA: Western Association of Schools and Colleges. 48 pp.

This manual contains specific WASC standards as well as practical guidance for any institution starting out in assessment. Included are implementing a WASC-oriented initiative and principles of good practice in assessment. Appendices include a compendium of WASC standards assessing institutional effectiveness, information sources for assessment, application of the principles, alternative ways of initiating assessment efforts, and assessment and accreditation. AR, MT, OA, TH

4. ACT. (1994). Motivating students for successful outcomes assessment. Iowa City, IA: Author. 36 pp.

This document discusses fundamental principles for motivating students to take assessments seriously and work effectively when being assessed. Appendices contain brochures and other materials from various institutions used to communicate with students about assessment. EX, M, MO, MT, PR, SC, TH

5. Adelman, Clifford (Ed.). (1986). Assessment in American higher education: Issues and contexts. Office of Educational Research and Improvement Publication OR86-301. Washington, DC: U. S. Department of Education. 82 pp.

This series of six papers by various authors reviews the status of outcome assessment in American higher education and the costs of assessment and provides practical instruction about assessment and resources for practitioners. CA, MT, S, TH

6. Adelman, Clifford (Ed.). (1988). Performance and judgment: Essays on principles and practice in the assessment of college student learning. Office of Educational Research and Improvement Publication OR88-514. Washington, DC: U. S. Department of Education. 325 pp.

This book gathers in one place information valuable to academicians new to assessment that is otherwise found scattered through diverse professional literatures. Seventeen chapters by ten different experts include such diverse topics as designing a college assessment; assessing generic outcomes, basic skills, language, general education, the major field of study, change in student values, and motivation; the concept of value added; computer-based testing; writing and other performance assessments; and the assessment center. The book concludes with an annotated bibliography and data on selected assessment instruments. A, AC, BI, CD, CT, E, EV, GE, GN, H, IN, IS, M, MO, MT, OA, PR, T, TC, TH, VA, W

7. Adelman, Clifford (Ed.). (1989). *Signs & traces: Model indicators of college student learning in the disciplines.* Office of Educational Research and Improvement Publication OR89-538. Washington, DC: U.S. Department of Education. 173 pp.

This volume reviews means of assessing student learning in specific disciplines: computer science, mechanical engineering, biology, physics, and chemistry. Although oriented to natural science and technology, there is much generic information useful in other, non-science disciplines as well. An introduction by the editor provides an overview of indicators (measures) and problems in their use, and the philosophy of the volume. DI, IN, IS, M, MT, O, OA, PS, TH

8. Advisory Committee to the College Outcomes Evaluation Program. (1987). *Report to the New Jersey Board of Higher Education from the Advisory Committee to the College Outcomes Evaluation Program.* Trenton, NJ: New Jersey Department of Higher Education. 30 pp., Appendix 147 pp.

This report, which led to the establishment of the statewide New Jersey COEP assessment effort, consists of an overview of the Program (the "Green Book") and appendices (the "Blue Book"). Together, these documents summarize the results of two years of study by several statewide committees of faculty members, administrators, and citizens and contain much valuable information for any institution, system, or state system developing an assessment program. Components of the Program included a statewide test of higher-order thinking skills (the *New Jersey General Intellectual Skills Assessment*—now available as the ETS *Tasks in Critical Thinking*); general education; the major field of concentration; student personal development; retention of students on campus, student satisfaction, and related variables; faculty research, scholarship, and creative expression; and community and societal impact. The appendix includes detailed recommendations of four specialized subcommittees, background evidence, and summaries of the committees' work. A, AY, CD, CS, CT, G, GE, M, MS, MT, O, OA, PG, RS, SS, SW, TH

9. Aleamoni, Lawrence M. (Ed.). (1987). *Techniques for evaluating and improving instruction.* New Directions for Teaching and Learning, No. 31. San Francisco: Jossey-Bass. 96 pp.

Nine chapters by various authors explore ways of evaluating and improving teaching. Topics include the role of evaluation of instruction in improving teaching, ways to help faculty accept new ideas, faculty concerns about student evaluations, use of student ratings to improve instruction, the role of student government in faculty evaluation, formative and summative evaluation, instructional evaluation as feedback, a faculty evaluation model for commu-

nity and junior colleges, and practical approaches for faculty and administrators. The editor draws together unifying ideas at the end, and a final chapter provides additional sources of information. BI, CC, EI, FA, FE, SE, U

10. Alexander, Lawrence T., & Davis, Robert H. (1977). *Writing useful instructional objectives.* (Guides for the Improvement of Instruction in Higher Education No. 1.) East Lansing, MI: Michigan State University. 12 pp.

This guide defines course-level outcomes in the form of instructional objectives. (For source see Davis and Alexander, 1977.) C, G, O, OS

11. Alfred, Richard L. (1994). Measuring teaching effectiveness. In Terry O'Banion & Associates (Eds.), *Teaching & learning in the community college* (pp. 263-283). Washington, DC: American Association of Community Colleges.

This article describes the elements of effective teaching, variables affecting teaching quality, essential organizational characteristics that permit effective teaching, and key elements of faculty evaluation. CC, EI, U

12. Allegre, Marla, & Guista, Michael. (1993). What every English teacher ought to know about using student evaluations. *Teaching English in the Two-Year College, 20,* 57-63.

This article reviews research on student evaluations of teaching, both across-the-curriculum and in writing classes. The authors discuss the different needs of evaluation for professional development and for promotion. DI, EI

13. Alverno College. (1979). *The volunteer assessor at Alverno College.* Milwaukee, WI: Alverno Productions. 10 pp.

This booklet describes the use of off-campus assessors in the Alverno College assessment of undergraduate students. A, AC, EX, FE, G, GE, O, OA, SU, TH, U

14. Alverno College Faculty. (1979). *Assessment at Alverno College.* Milwaukee, WI: Alverno Productions. 60 pp.

In Alverno College's outcome-based curricula, assessment is at every point an integral component of the educational process. This booklet describes in detail the process of assessment at Alverno. CR, EX, FE, G, GE, MT, O, OA, SU, TH, U

15. Anderson, Erin. (1993). Campus use of the teaching portfolio: Twenty-five profiles. Washington, DC: American Association for Higher Education Teaching Initiative. 122 pp.

This monograph, which includes an introduction by Pat Hutchings, Director, AAHE Teaching Initiatives, is a companion piece to *The teaching portfolio: Capturing the scholarship in teaching* (see Edgerton, 1991). The profiles of campus practice provide detailed but concise accounts of what twenty-five campuses are doing with and learning about portfolios. Each profile includes contextual information about the particular campus and addresses a common set of issues, including portfolio content and evaluation. EI, EX, FA, PT, SF

16. Anderson, Scarvia B., Ball, Samuel, Murphy, Richard T., & Associates. (1975). *Encyclopedia of educational evaluation.* San Francisco: Jossey-Bass. 515 pp.

This comprehensive encyclopedia of concepts of educational assessment and evaluation includes 142 articles in the following categories: evaluation models, functions and targets of evaluation, program objectives and standards, social context of evaluation, planning and design, systems technology, variables, measurement approaches and types, technical measurement considerations, reactive concerns, and analysis and interpretation. Each article contains a narrative followed by a short, briefly annotated bibliography of important works. The volume concludes with a 24-page bibliography. BI, E, EV, GN, HP, TH

17. Angelo, Thomas A. (Ed.). (1991). *Classroom research: Early lessons from success.* New Directions for Teaching and Learning, No. 46. San Francisco: Jossey-Bass. 134 pp.

Ten chapters by various authors introduce classroom research (CR); describe examples of quickly usable methods; provide examples from composition, accounting, a large introductory science course, psychology, and physics; describe a campuswide CR project in a state university, using cooperative learning and CR with culturally diverse students; and implementing and maintaining a CR project in a community college. C, CC, DI, DV, I, MT, SR, TH, U, W

18. Angelo, Thomas A. (1994). Transformative faculty development: Realizing the promise through classroom research. In Terry O'Banion & Associates (Eds.), *Teaching & learning in the community college* (pp. 115-142). Washington, DC: American Association of Community Colleges.

This article describes principles for using classroom research to improve the professional development of college faculty members by focusing attention on student learning. The author defines classroom research and assessment and describes environmental pressures on colleges that require significant improvement in faculty professional knowledge and skills. C, CC, FE, U

19. Angelo, Thomas A. (1995, April). Reassessing assessment: Embracing contraries, bridging gaps, and resetting the agenda. *AAHE Bulletin, 47*(8), 10-13.

This article points out contradictions and gaps in assessment as it is commonly practiced on campuses and suggests redefining assessment as a means for achieving several different important ends in institutions. (See also Angelo, 1995, November.) AY, HP, IW, SC

20. Angelo, Thomas A. (1995, November). Reassessing (and defining) assessment. *AAHE Bulletin, 48*(3), 7-9.

This article reviews responses to the author's article earlier in the year (Angelo, 1995, April) concerning reassessing assessment and proposes a redefinition of assessment. AY, IW, SC, TH

21. Angelo, Thomas A., & Cross, K. Patricia. (1993). *Classroom assessment techniques: A handbook for college teachers.* San Francisco: Jossey-Bass. 427 pp.

In this handbook for assessment in the classroom, the authors introduce classroom assessment (CA), justify its importance, and offer seven basic assumptions of CA. They describe first steps to take, ways to plan and implement CA projects, and twelve examples of successful CA projects in various disciplines. Detailed descriptions are provided of 50 classroom assessment techniques (CATs) for assessing course-related knowledge and skills; learner attitudes, values, and self-awareness; and learner reactions to instruction. Two final chapters describe what was learned in six years of CA and next steps in CA and classroom research. Five appendices include a list of institutions which developed the Teaching Goals Inventory (TGI), the TGI and self-scorable worksheet, comparative data on the TGI in community colleges and four-year colleges, and a bibliography of resources on classroom research and assessment. A, BI, C, CD, CT, DI, EI, EX, G, H, I, IS, MT, OA, TH, U

22. Arreola, Raoul A. (1995). *Developing a comprehensive faculty evaluation system: A handbook for college faculty and administrators on designing and operating a comprehensive faculty evaluation system.* Bolton, MA: Anker. 191 pp.

This handbook discusses key issues in beginning and eight steps for developing a faculty evaluation system. Each step deals with specific technical issues, tools and procedures, and use of the system, including for promotion and tenure and merit pay calculations. Issues include portfolio systems, peer evaluation methods, types of student evaluation rating systems, administration of student evaluation rating systems, and the relationship between faculty evaluation and faculty development. Four chapters, which constitute a "student rating form development kit," discuss common misconceptions and beliefs, published forms, and techniques for designing a form, and include a catalog of 504 rating items dealing with 24 different aspects of a course. An appendix contains a sample evaluation manual. An extensive bibliography completes the book. BI, EI, FA, H, IN, IS, MT, PA, PR, PT, SF, TC, TH, U

23. Ashworth, Kenneth H. (1994, November/December). Performance-based funding in higher education: The Texas case study. *Change, 26*(6), 8-15.

The commissioner of the Texas Higher Education Coordinating Board describes the Board's response to a legislative directive to develop a performance funding plan for the state system of higher education. The model includes teaching, research, and public service goals and 13 specific indicators of quality. AY, G, IN, IW, OA, PI, SW

24. *Assessing the outcomes of higher education.* (1986, October 25). Paper presented at the ETS Invitational Conference, New York. 110 pp.

These presentations introduce outcome assessment in American higher education and focus on the aims and realities of college-level learning; college, state, and accrediting association perspectives on the why, what, and who of assessment; key validity issues for assessment; the importance of unobtrusive measures; using assessment to improve instruction; and the relative value of value-added assessment. AR, EV, OA, SW, VA

25. Astin, Alexander W. (1991). *Assessment for excellence: The philosophy and practice of assessment and evaluation in higher education.* Phoenix, AZ: Oryx. 335 pp.

This comprehensive textbook on assessment in higher education discusses the philosophy and logic of assessment and provides a conceptual assessment model. Instruction is provided for assessing outcomes, inputs, and the educational environment; analyzing assessment data; and using the results of assessment to improve quality of the learning environment. Other chapters describe construction of a database, assessment as direct feedback to students, assessment and equity and public policy, and the future of assessment. An appendix that discusses the statistical analysis of longitudinal data provides a very basic review of statistical concepts such as means, standard deviations, correlation, simple and multiple regression, assessing environmental effects, and causal modeling. DB, EX, EV, FA, H, HP, MT, ST, TH, U, VA

26. Astin, Alexander W. (1993). *What matters in college? Four critical years revisited.* San Francisco: Jossey-Bass. 482 pp.

A follow-up on the author's 1977 study, *Four Critical Years,* this book reports the findings of a major study of college effects on students using a variety of sources of data from almost 25,000 students, hundreds of faculty members, and 309 colleges and universities. Astin studied the impact on 82 outcome measures of 146 student input measures and 192 college environmental measures, including 57 of degree of student involvement. This study provides a model for understanding student development in college; can suggest outcome, process, and input variables to assess; and shows how to handle this type of study methodologically. A, BI, CD, CG, CM, CT, DV, E, EL, ET, GE, I, IA, MT, OA, PA, RR, ST, SU, TH

27. Baird, Leonard L. (1985). Do grades and tests predict adult accomplishment? *Research in Higher Education, 23,* 3-85.

This major study focuses on the predictive validity of college grades. It reviews the literature on the relationship of academic ability and grades among high school students, college students, and people who performed at a very high level in their fields. GR, RR

28. Ball, Robert, & Halwachi, Jalil. (1987). Performance indicators in higher education. *Higher Education, 16,* 303-405.

The authors discuss the use of performance indicators to evaluate institutions of higher education, stressing the importance of clear goals for such indicators to be useful, and describe problems encountered when using such indicators. (ERIC) AY, IW, MT, PI, PR

29. Banta, Trudy W. (Ed.). (1986). *Performance funding in higher education: A critical analysis of Tennessee's experience.* Boulder, CO: National Center for Higher Education Management Systems. 175 pp.

This book provides an account of the experience of the University of Tennessee-Knoxville in responding to the performance funding program of the State of Tennessee. Administrators, faculty members, and assessment experts describe various aspects of UTK's response and lessons from the experience. Six appendices contain the state Standards of Performance, variables and standards for evaluating instruction, an excerpt from a student satisfaction survey, and guidelines for self-study. AR, AY, GE, IW, M, PE, PI, PL, RU, SS, SW

30. Banta, Trudy W. (Ed.). (1988). *Implementing outcomes assessment: Promise and perils.* New Directions for Institutional Research, No. 59. San Francisco: Jossey-Bass. 112 pp.

Nine chapters by various authors discuss the use of knowledge of change processes in complex organizations to gain acceptance of assessment, key organizational considerations in assessment, the embedding of program evaluation items in course-level examinations, the use of noncognitive measures, issues to consider when measuring value added, costs of assessment, assessment as a component of funding policy, and use of broad-based assessment programs. A final chapter constitutes an annotated bibliography and a description of assessment programs. AY, BI, C, CA, EX, IW, MO, MT, OA, PR, SC, SW, TH, VA

31. Banta, Trudy W. (1991). Contemporary approaches to assessing student achievement of general education outcomes. *Journal of General Education, 40,* 203-223.

Using examples from various institutions and states, the author reviews the development of efforts to assess outcomes during the first five years of the assessment movement. She discusses the limitations of standardized tests in general, specifically critiquing several commercially available instruments, and stresses the importance of starting any outcome assessment effort by defining outcome goals clearly. The book concludes with assessment strategies and lessons from experience with assessment. CU, EX, G, HP, IS, MT, OA, ST, SW, TD

32. Banta, Trudy W. (1991). *Toward a plan for using national assessment to ensure continuous improvement of higher education.* Knoxville, TN: University of Tennessee. (ERIC Document Reproduction Service No. ED 340 753)

This paper was commissioned by the U.S. Department of Education as background for a study design workshop for a national assessment of college student learning held in November 1991. It enumerates five assumptions that underpin National Education Goal 6.5 and suggests that "under prevailing conditions in American higher education, little support for these assumptions exists." The author suggests that concepts of Continuous Quality Improvement should be employed to connect goals, educational improvement, and assessment in a systematic way. This report includes the comments of two respondents. (ERIC) BI, NT, OA

33. Banta, Trudy W. (1992). Selected references on outcomes assessment in higher education: An annotated bibliography. In *Accreditation, assessment and institutional effectiveness: Resource papers for the COPA Task Force on Institutional Effectiveness* (pp. 57-68). Washington, DC: Council on Postsecondary Accreditation.

These key references provide accrediting agency staff and others an overview of the current status of outcomes assessment and assessment of institutional effectiveness. Annotations are provided for all references in the 12 sections of the bibliography. AR, B, C, CC, EV, G, GE, M, MT, OA, SU, SW, TH

34. Banta, Trudy W., & Associates. (1993). *Making a difference: Outcomes of a decade of assessment in higher education.* San Francisco: Jossey-Bass. 388 pp.

Twenty-four chapters describing assessment activities are divided into five sections: Transforming Campus Cultures Through Assessment, Adapting Assessment to Diverse Settings and Populations, Outcomes Assessment Methods That Work, Approaches with Promise for Improving Programs and Services, and State-Level Approaches to Assessment. Practitioners on individual campuses author chapters that describe their work. The book includes descriptions of common approaches to assessment such as portfolios, cognitive and affective measures, the Community College Student Experiences Questionnaire, classroom assessment, assessment centers, student self-evaluation, Total Quality Management, and assessment of general education and the major. State-level issues include performance funding, the New Jersey COEP program, and the role of states and accreditors in shaping assessment. In a final chapter Banta suggests that if permitted to reach its potential, assessment may make "a greater difference for students than any other single influence in the history of higher education" (p. 375). A, AC, AR, AY, C, CC, CE, CQ, EX, GE, HP, IS, M, MT, OA, P, PA, PG, RU, S, SA, SC, SW, TR, U

35. Banta, Trudy W., & Fisher, Homer S. (1990, October). An international perspective on assessing baccalaureate program outcomes. *Evaluation Practice, 11*(3), 167-175.

The authors review similarities and differences among the systems of higher education in western nations, describe a "universal concern about accountability," and briefly compare methods for assessing the abilities of baccalaureate-level graduates. AR, AY, IT, OA

36. Banta, Trudy W., Lambert, E. Warren, Pike, Gary R., Schmidhammer, James L., & Schneider, Janet A. (1987). Estimated student score gain on the ACT COMP exam: Valid tool for institutional assessment? *Research in Higher Education, 27*(3), 195-217.

A study of the gains in scores across the undergraduate years on the ACT COMP examination raised "grave doubts" as to the validity and reliability of gain scores on this assessment and thus their usefulness as measures of value added to students by institutions' general education curricula. The specific causes of concern are discussed in detail. EV, EX, GE, IN, IS, MT, OA, PR, RU, ST, TC, TH, U, VA

37. Banta, Trudy W., Lund, Jon P., Black, Karen E., & Oblander, Frances W. (1996). *Assessment in practice: Putting principles to work on college campuses.* San Francisco: Jossey-Bass. 387 pp.

The authors devote a chapter to each of the nine AAHE Principles of Good Practice for Assessing Student Learning (AAHE Assessment Forum, 1992) and add one of their own. A second, major part of the book consists of 82 specific cases written by faculty and student-affairs staff members whose campus-based assessment projects embody the nine principles. Included are examples of capstone course assessment, senior assignment, sophomore-junior diagnostic project, postgraduate assessment, assessment of general education and the major, use of portfolios, licensure assessment, exit interviews, student projects, assessment of the honors program, using student development transcripts, and assessment of academic advising. Banta concludes that assessment has proved successful in some institutions, holds promise in others, but needs better reporting to satisfy supporters and detractors of higher education. A, AA, BI, EX, G, GE, LI, M, MO, MT, OA, P, PA, PE, PG, TE, TR, U, VA, W

38. Banta, Trudy W., & Pike, Gary R. (1989). Methods for comparing outcomes assessment instruments. *Research in Higher Education, 30*(5), 455-469.

This guide for faculty members is useful in comparing instruments for assessing students' achievement of outcome goals in general education. Using the ACT COMP and a pilot version of the ETS Academic Profile, the authors describe the instruments, content analyses of the instruments, student reactions to the instruments (judgment of degree of coverage, level of interest, and degree to which they had worked to full capacity), and statistical analyses (validity and reliability). Among other conclusions, the authors state that "student motivation to perform conscientiously on tests required for purposes of assessment must be considered a major concern" (p. 467). DV, GE, I, IS, MO, MT, OA, RU, TC

39. Barak, Robert J., & Breier, Barbara E. (1990). *Successful program review: A practical guide to evaluating programs in academic settings.* San Francisco: Jossey-Bass. 139 pp.

This handbook for program review discusses establishing objectives and principles of program review; planning and conducting the review; analyzing, communicating, and applying the results of review; defining roles of faculty, institutional support, administrators, trustees, and state-agency staff; and linking program reviews to institutional assessment, accreditation, and planning. AC, AY, H, MT, PE, PL, U

40. Barak, Robert J., & Mets, Lisa A. (Eds.). (1995). *Using academic program review.* New Directions for Institutional Research, No. 86. San Francisco: Jossey-Bass. 96 pp.

This book discusses how to use academic program review in planning, budgeting, assessment, and academic departments, and how to use organizational variables in program review. One chapter provides a system-wide perspective on program review at the University of Maryland. A final chapter provides a literature review, synthesis of experience, and factors critical to successful use of program review. AY, BI, CC, CO, D, PE, RU

41. Barrow, John, Cox, Patti, Sepich, Rob, & Spival, Rene. (1989). Student needs assessment surveys: Do they predict student use of service? *Journal of College Student Development, 30,* 77-82.

This study explored the relationship between surveys assessing student needs and subsequent use of services. In the context of a counseling center, survey information was only "modestly indicative" of student interest in group and workshop services. The authors conclude that one measure is not sufficient to determine students' needs. Multiple sources and on-going assessment are necessary. Included are suggestions for creating informative and useful needs assessment. D, NA, SN

42. Barton, Paul E., & Lapointe, Archie. (1995). *Learning by degrees: Indicators of performance in higher education.* Princeton, NJ: Educational Testing Service, Policy Information Center. 85 pp.

This report summarizes the rationale, methodology, and results of the National Adult Literacy Survey of 25,000 adults aged 16 or over, conducted in 1992 and designed to provide information in support of achievement of National Education Goal 5.5 (now 6.5), regarding cognitive outcomes. The report summarizes already known data about the outcomes of college learning based on GRE and GMAT scores. AY, CD, CT, GE, I, IN, MT, NT, OA, PG, PI, RR

43. Battersby, James L. (1973). *Typical folly: Evaluating student performance in higher education.* Urbana, IL: National Council of Teachers of English. 64 pp.

This piece discusses problems inherent in grades and alternatives to grades and proposes using written reports of student performance. GR

44. Beeler, Karl J., & Hunter, Deborah E. (Eds.). (1991). *Puzzles and pieces in wonderland: The promise and practice of student affairs research.* Washington, DC: National Association of Student Personnel Administrators. 142 pp.

Using an allegorical reference to *Alice's Adventures in Wonderland*, this monograph is written as a practical approach to research and assessment in student affairs. The editors present an overview of the importance of conducting student affairs research on college and university campuses. Throughout, research and assessment are presented as interesting, affordable, manageable, and necessary guides to decision making and accountability. Strategies for conducting research and conventional and naturalistic modes of inquiry are discussed. CA, G, GN, I, MT, OA, SN

45. Bers, Trudy H. (1992). The costs and benefits of student tracking systems. *AACJC Journal, 62*(4), 20-23.

Tracking is "the systematic gathering, analysis, and communication of information on where students have been and are now with respect to their academic skills, progress toward a degree, and subsequent employment or transfer after leaving the particular college" (p. 21). Tracking systems and their required data bases are essential for understanding student progress and institutional educational effectiveness. The author describes the purposes and audience for tracking; organizational issues in developing and using a tracking system; uses of data, benefits and costs of tracking systems; and the importance of realistic expectations and clear purposes. CA, CC, DV, T

46. Bers, Trudy H., & Smith, Kerry E. (1990). Assessing assessment programs: The theory and practice of examining reliability and validity of a writing placement test. *Community College Review, 18*(3), 17-27.

This article reports the methodology and results of a study designed to determine the validity and reliability of a writing placement test. BS, CC, DI, MT, PC, TC, TH, W

47. Bess, James L. (1979). Classroom and management decisions using student data: Designing an information system. *Journal of Higher Education, 50*(3), 256-279.

This review of the status of what colleges and universities know about their students provides suggestions of ways of understanding them and using the information they develop. An appendix contains an extensive listing of assessment instruments cited throughout the paper. IS, OA

48. Blanzy, James J., & Sucher, Joseph E. (1992, January 27). *Technology: The silent partner in the advancement of measurement and assessment practices (A student centered assessment model).* Paper presented at the Winter Institute on Community College Effectiveness and Student Success, Jacksonville, FL. 8 pp. (ERIC Document Reproduction Service No. ED 342 446)

The authors describe the computer-based system at Macomb Community College (MI) for tracking student progress through the college experience. Based on six assumptions about students and learning, the five-part model includes (1) analysis of placement test scores, course grades, and placement recommendations to judge comparative success and retention rates of students, (2) early warning system for students in the first weeks of courses, (3) long-term monitoring of student programs, (4) exit competency assessment, including measurement of gains across the college experience, and (5) transfer and employment information to improve the educational process. CC, DB, EX, IR, MT, PL, T, U

49. Bloland, Paul A., & Others. (1994). *Reform in student affairs: A critique of student development.* Greensboro, NC: ERIC Clearinghouse on Counseling and Student Services. 115 pp. (ERIC Document Reproduction Service No. ED 366 862)

This monograph provides an intensive examination of the student development movement in college student affairs. Specifically, Chapter III raises a number of significant questions regarding current student development theories and their implementation on the college campus, employing six criteria of effective theory as an assessment template. The monograph concludes with an alternative paradigm for the student affairs field that places it firmly within the mission of higher education while avoiding problems noted in evaluation of the fledgling paradigm of student development. (ERIC) FR, SN, SU

50. Bloom, Benjamin S. (Ed.). (1956). *Taxonomy of educational objectives: The classification of educational goals. Handbook 1: Cognitive domain.* New York: Longman. 207 pp.

This classic is used by teachers to control the cognitive level in outcomes statements (objectives), classes, assignments, and assessments. Its six levels of cognitive demand describe types of cognitive operations required to answer a question, complete an assignment, or respond to an assessment task. An historical review, a description of the three domains of learning and the development of the cognitive domain precede chapters on the taxonomy and its development, educational objectives and development of curriculum, and problems when classifying objectives and test items. Over two-thirds of the book describes each level of the Taxonomy, including typical behaviors and test items for each level. An appendix contains a condensed version of the taxonomy, without detailed explanatory material. (Also see Krathwohl et al., 1964, for the companion taxonomy in the affective domain and Harrow, 1972, for an unrelated taxonomy for the psychomotor domain.) C, CD, CU, H, HP, I, MT, O, OA, OS, PR, TA, TH

51. Bloom, Benjamin S., Hastings, J. Thomas, & Madaus, George F. (1971). *Handbook on formative and summative evaluation of student learning.* New York: McGraw-Hill. 923 pp.

This classic describes the uses of assessment as an aid to student learning in courses. *Part 1.* Sections include defining learning outcomes as objectives and mastery learning; summative evaluation, assessment for placement and diagnosis, and formative evaluation; assessment for knowledge and comprehension, application and analysis, synthesis and evaluation, and affective objectives; and cooperative development of assessment systems and emerging developments. An appendix contains a condensed version of the Taxonomy of Educational Objectives. *Part 2.* Eleven chapters, all by different authors, and primarily directed to the K-12 sector, discuss assessment in various disciplines. A discussion of tables of specifications for designing assessment indicators provides disparate examples of assessment blueprints. A, FE, IN, O, OA, SE, TA, TS

52. Bogue, E. Grady, & Saunders, Robert L. (1992). *The Evidence for quality: Strengthening the tests of academic and administrative effectiveness.* San Francisco: Jossey-Bass. 313 pp.

This book summarizes major ways to judge the quality of institutions. Seven chapters review accreditation, rankings and ratings of reputation, post-graduation studies, professional licensure, academic program review, and assessment of outcomes. Three additional chapters discuss improving quality by forming partnerships with states, adopting quality assurance methods, and developing a strategic vision of quality. AD, AR, EX, HP, LI, OA, PE, PG, RA, TA

53. Borden, Victor M. H., & Banta, Trudy W. (Eds.). (1994). *Using performance indicators to guide strategic decision making.* New Directions for Institutional Research, No. 82. San Francisco: Jossey-Bass. 124 pp.

Seven chapters by various authors describe the historical background, definitions, and methods of using performance indicators; the development and use of data and indicators at the National Center for Higher Education Management Systems; performance indicators and quality assurance in European higher education; a Total Quality Management perspective on assessing the performance of institutions; the use of performance indicators in strategic decision making; activity-based costing for assessing institutional economic performance; and the use of performance indicators for accountability and improvement. An appendix provides a master table of measures cited in the literature as examples of input, process, and output indicators. AY, BI, CQ, EX, HP, IA, IN, IR, IW, MT, OA, PA, PL, S, TC

54. Boud, David. (1989). The role of self-assessment in student grading. *Assessment and Evaluation in Higher Education, 14*(1), 20-30.

This paper contends that student self-assessment is both a device for enhancing learning and for formal assessment. The author suggests two arguments in favor of self-assessment: students need to be able to assess themselves when they do not understand or agree with criteria of others (a "reality argument" for self-assessment) and when self-assessment reduces staff time devoted to assessment (the argument from "expediency"). After a literature review on student self-assessment, an evaluation of the available studies, and an analysis of implications for the use of self-assessment, the author offers seven ways to strengthen the validity, reliability, and usefulness of student self-assessment, with future directions for research. C, EV, FR, GR, I, SA, TC

55. Bowen, Howard R. (1979, December). Outcomes assessment—A new era in accreditation. *Proceedings of the Ninety-third Annual Convention of the Middle States Association of Colleges and Schools* (pp. 27-38). Philadelphia: Middle States Association of Colleges and Schools.

This keynote address sets out the rationale for clear goals and the assessment of outcomes in higher education. In the context of accreditation and accountability, the author, a college president, urges the use of new, more sophisticated methods of managing colleges and universities and contrasts these methods with current practices. AR, AY, G, MG, OA

56. Boyer, Carol M., Ewell, Peter T., Finney, Joni E., & Mingle, James R. (1987, March). Assessment and outcomes measurement: A view from the states. *AAHE Bulletin, 39*(7), 8-12.

This article is a summary of a 50-state survey of assessment activity in the states, sponsored by ECS, AAHE, and SHEEO. (Also see Ewell and Boyer, 1988.) OA, SW

57. Braskamp, Larry A., & Ory, John C. (1994). *Assessing faculty work: Enhancing individual and institutional performance.* San Francisco: Jossey-Bass. 333 pp.

This book reviews the current status of faculty assessment and links faculty assessment and development. Sections discuss setting expectations; collecting, organizing, and using assessment evidence; and specific methods of collecting evidence concerning faculty work. Thirteen resource sections provide a faculty development plan and numerous assessment methods and tools, including assessment instruments. BI, EI, FA, IN, IS, MT, PA, SF, TH

58. Bray, Dorothy, & Belcher, Marcia J. (Eds.). (1987). *Issues in student assessment.* New Directions for Community Colleges, No. 59. San Francisco: Jossey-Bass. 122 pp.

Twelve chapters by various authors explore aspects of assessment. Chapters describe the spread of assessment in American education, assessment for accountability and for improving education, value-added assessment, teacher-made tests, a writing assessment program, placement testing, making accommodations for disabled students, the impact of assessment on minority student access, and technology and assessment. A final chapter provides additional resources. C, CC, DV, EX, HP, OA, PC, T, VA, W

59. Brinkman, Paul T. (Ed.). (1987). *Conducting interinstitutional comparisons.* New Directions for Institutional Research, No. 53. San Francisco: Jossey-Bass. 112 pp.

Seven chapters by various authors discuss considerations when selecting comparison groups, sources of comparative data, establishing a project for sharing data, using comparative data within an institution, system- and state-level analysis, financial analysis, and the importance of planning and effort for producing useful comparisons. AY, EX, IW, MT, PR, SW, TH

60. Brown, Sally, Rush, Chris, & Gibbs, Graham. (1994). *Strategies for diversifying assessment in higher education.* Oxford, England: The Oxford Centre for Staff Development. 52 pp.

A general guide to assessment, this workbook explores standards, criteria, and methods of assessment. It also addresses the role of students in assessment and includes examples to illustrate the concepts. The workbook was written to accompany workshops conducted by the Oxford Centre for Staff Development, but may be used alone. C, GN, MT, SD, SS

61. Butler, Richard P, Wilson, William L., & Priest, Robert F. (1984, November). *Description, evaluation, and validation of a pilot developmental assessment center in a military-educational environment.* Paper presented at the 26th Annual Conference of the Military Testing Association, Munich, Germany. (ERIC Document Reproduction Service No. ED 251 511)

This presentation describes a pilot assessment center at the United States Military Academy and its evaluation and validation procedures. Cadets were individually tested for twelve leadership skills and provided with individual feedback on their strengths and weaknesses. AC, I, OA, SI

62. Capelli, Peter. (1991). *Assessing college education: What can be learned from practices in industry.* Philadelphia: University of Pennsylvania. 40 pp.

This paper was commissioned by the U.S. Department of Education as background for a study design workshop for a national assessment of college student learning held in November 1991. The author applies what has been learned about describing jobs and testing competence in industry to the assessment of college graduates' learning in college. (ERIC) I, MT, NT, OA

63. Carey, Lou M. (1994). *Measuring and evaluating school learning.* Boston: Allyn and Bacon. 534 pp.

This general textbook on measurement and evaluation in education, although oriented to the classroom teacher, is a basic handbook on theory and practice in the field. The book's four parts are linking testing and instruction, designing and using objective tests, designing and using alternative assessments (essay, product development, active performance tests, tests for non-readers, portfolios, and mastery charts), and communicating student progress. This volume contains a thorough discussion of assessment blueprints or tables of specification for designing assessments. C, EV, G, GR, H, I, MT, O, OS, PR, ST, TA, TH

64. Caruthers, J. K., & Lott, G. B. (1981). *Mission review: Foundation for strategic planning.* Boulder, CO: National Center for Higher Education Management Systems. 188 pp.

This handbook for planning a review of institutional mission statements is set in the context of strategic planning. Chapters include a review of planning in higher education, the mission review as a foundation for planning and decision making, contents of mission statements, and conducting a mission review. A second part gives the mission statement and abstracts of three-year strategic plans for a large state research university. A supplement discusses state-level mission review. EX, H, MS, SP, SW

65. Cashin, William E. (1987, January). *Improving essay tests* (IDEA Paper No. 17). Manhattan, KS: Kansas State University, Center for Faculty Evaluation and Development. 4 pp.

This leaflet provides practical suggestions for improving the effectiveness of essay examinations. To obtain copies call (800) 255-2757. C, OA

66. Cave, Martin, Hanney, Stephen, & Kogan, Maurice. (1991). *The use of performance indicators in higher education: A critical analysis of developing practice.* Higher Education Policy Series 3. London: Jessica Kingsley. 192 pp.

This book reviews issues in the development of performance indicators such as policy background, central control versus institutional autonomy, defining performance indicators, and assessment; provides a comparative overview of the use of performance indicators in Great Britain, the United States, and other countries; reviews the literature on performance indicators of educational effectiveness, including the concept of value-added and of research performance; and summarizes the types, models, and ways in which performance indicators have been used by funding agencies, institutions, and departments. AY, BI, IA, IR, IT, IW, MT, OA, PA, PI, PR, VA

67. Chamberlain, Don, Gordon, Gus, & Plunkett, Linda. (1994, August). Auditors in the academic domain: Using internal auditors for academic assessment. *NACUBO Business Officer, 28*(2), 31-34.

The authors argue that an institution's professional internal auditors who are broadly trained to understand the institution and its units as systemic wholes can contribute to the process of assessing and evaluating the performance of academic departments. AY, D, GN, PE

68. Clegg, Victoria L., & Cashin, William E. (1986, September). *Improving multiple-choice tests* (IDEA Paper No. 16). Manhattan, KS: Kansas State University, Center for Faculty Evaluation and Development. 4 pp.

This leaflet provides a compact summary of practical suggestions for improving the effectiveness of multiple-choice tests in courses. To obtain copies call (800) 255-2757. C, EV, I, OA

69. College Board. (1983). *Academic preparation for college: What students need to know and be able to do.* New York: Author. 46 pp.

This volume, sometimes known as the "Green Book," describes competencies students should bring to college. The College Board has also published six discipline-specific books of outcomes that expand on this volume. H, OA, SS, TH

70. Commission on Colleges. (1987). *Resource manual on institutional effectiveness.* Atlanta, GA: Southern Association of Colleges and Schools. 36 pp.

This booklet provides an overview of processes for improving institutional effectiveness. Included are philosophy and rationale, planning and evaluation, ways to manage the process, and comments on quality in higher education. Three appendices contain information on assessment of current practice, examples of planning and evaluation processes, and a bibliography. AR, H, IE, IW, PL, TH

71. Council for the Advancement of Standards in Higher Education. (1997). *CAS standards and guidelines* (Rev. 2nd ed.). Washington, DC: Author.

CAS has established standards and guidelines for 23 functional areas of higher education programs and services. Additionally, Masters Level Standards for Student Affairs Preparation Programs exist for program review use. The CAS Standards provide measures of program and service effectiveness, designs for program and service development and assessment, criteria for institutional self-studies and preparation for accreditation, opportunities for staff development, directions for student learning and development, and frameworks for accountability. Available through Carmen G. Neuberger, CAS Treasurer, c/o American College Personnel Association, One Dupont Circle, NW, Suite 300, Washington, DC 20036-1110, ph. (202) 835-2272. AY, D, PE, SA, SS

72. Corallo, Sal. (1996). *The national assessment of college student learning: An inventory of state-level assessment activities: A report of the proceedings of the third study design workshop* (NCES 96-862). Washington, DC: U.S. Department of Education, Office of Educational Research and Improvement, National Center for Education Statistics. 152 pp.

This report describes state-level efforts and plans for assessment of college student learning gleaned from a 1995 inventory and a workshop of assessment experts. Although more states were doing assessment in 1995 than in 1989, their political concerns shifted from improving undergraduate education to issues of governance and finance. The report discusses assessment efforts of each state and conclusions of workshop participants about issues in developing, administering, and interpreting the future of state- and national-level assessment. A, AY, CD, CE, CT, FR, GE, HP, IC, IN, NT, OA, PG, PR, S, SS, SW, TC

73. Corallo, Sal, & Fisher, Gayle. (1992). *National assessment of college student learning: Issues and concerns* (NCES 92-068). Washington, DC: U.S. Department of Education, Office of Educational Research and Improvement, National Center for Education Statistics. 118 pp.

This report of a study design workshop in November 1991 considers issues in designing a national assessment of college student learning connected to the National Education Goal on Literacy and Adult Learning. Four work groups of experts responded to 17 commissioned papers about a national assessment and reviewers' comments on these papers. This report includes summaries of work group deliberations and comments from individual participants. AY, CD, CT, GE, IS, NT, OA, PG, S, TH, U

74. Cronbach, Lee J. (1984). *Essentials of psychological testing.* New York: Harper and Row. 630 pp.

This textbook includes understanding basic concepts of test design (users and purposes of tests), considering varieties of tests and interpretations, administering tests, scoring tests, validating tests, judging test quality, considering various types of ability, and establishing measures of typical performance such as interests and personality. Two appendices list sources of specialized tests and publishers and distributors of tests. A, BI, EV, GN, HB, IA, IS, MO, MT, PR, SC, ST, TC, TH, U

75. Cross, K. Patricia. (1993). Involving faculty in TQM. *AACC Journal, 63*(4), 15-20.

This is a briefer adaptation of Cross' chapter in *Teaching & Learning in the Community College* (Cross, 1994). C, CC, CQ, HP, U

76. Cross, K. Patricia. (1994). Involving faculty in TQM through classroom assessment. In Terry O'Banion & Associates (Eds.), *Teaching & learning in the community college* (pp. 143-159). Washington, DC: American Association of Community Colleges.

Cross reviews the introduction of TQM (CQI) into American higher education and shows in specific detail how classroom assessment can be powerfully used at numerous points to support an institution's TQM effort. C, CC, CQ, HP, U

77. Cross, K. Patricia, & Angelo, Thomas A. (1989). Faculty members as classroom researchers. *AACJC Journal, 59*(5), 23-25.

This is a brief description of classroom research and the development of the authors' Teaching Goals Inventory and handbook on practical classroom assessment methods. C, HP, U, X

78. Cross, K. Patricia, & Steadman, Mimi Harris. (1996). *Classroom research: Implementing the scholarship of teaching.* San Francisco: Jossey-Bass. 264 pp.

This volume, a companion to Cross' earlier *Classroom Assessment Techniques: A Handbook for Faculty* (Angelo and Cross, 1993), addresses teachers, students in graduate courses on learning and teaching, participants in faculty and teaching assistant development programs, and groups involved in classroom assessment and research. Three goals are to encourage and enable teachers to discuss teaching and learning together in a problem solving spirit, apply research findings to their own practice, and use classroom assessment and research with their own students. Focused on four cases written by teachers and illustrating practical issues of student learning, three chapters discuss prerequisite knowledge, metacognition and learning strategies, self-confidence and motivation, goals, deep versus surface learning, student ratings of instruction, peer learning, and cognitive development and critical thinking. For each case, a section presents hypotheses, key research applicable to the hypotheses, and examples of application of research to the hypotheses; refers to page numbers of relevant Classroom Assessment Techniques; and includes an annotated bibliography. A fourth chapter describes how to design classroom research in one's own courses. An extensive bibliography concludes the book. A, BI, C, CD, CT, EI, G, GR, H, OA,

79. Crowley, Mary L., & Dunn, Ken. (1995). The mathematics portfolio. *American Mathematical Monthly, 102*(1), 19-22.

The authors suggest how portfolios can be used with mathematics students. They include a list of categories of portfolio contents. D, DI, MT, OA

80. Davis, Robert H., & Alexander, Lawrence T. (1977). *Evaluating instruction* (Guides for the Improvement of Instruction in Higher Education No. 3). East Lansing, MI: Michigan State University. 28 pp.

This booklet helps teachers decide when they should evaluate the effectiveness of their instruction, why, and what data they will need. Order from Marketing Division, Instructional Media Center, Michigan State University, East Lansing 48824. ph. (517) 353-9229, fax (517) 353-1817. C, EI, PA

81. Deshler, David (Ed.). (1984). *Evaluation for program improvement.* New Directions for Continuing Education, No. 24. San Francisco: Jossey-Bass. 109 pp.

This collection of articles focuses on formative evaluation (evaluation for program improvement). The editor's introduction is followed by articles on constituencies in the evaluation process, formative evaluation as model building, evaluation of goals and purposes, value audits, formative evaluation in management training and organizational development, educational technology, the potential of monitoring programs, the theory of formative evaluation, and decision making. A, EX, FD, FE, G, O, PE, SC, T, TH

82. Donald, Janet G., & Denison, D. Brian. (1996). Evaluating undergraduate education: The use of broad indicators. *Assessment & Evaluation in Higher Education, 21*(1), 23-39.

Authors report the findings of a study on the utility of broad indicators of program quality for program improvement as contrasted with accountability. They discuss the strengths and weaknesses of such indicators. AY, IN, MT, PE, PG

83. Donald, Janet G., & Sullivan, Arthur M. (Eds.). (1985). *Using research to improve teaching.* New Directions for Teaching and Learning, No. 23. San Francisco: Jossey-Bass. 109 pp.

Seven chapters by various authors address means of improving instruction through research. Topics include the state of research on instructional effectiveness, classroom behaviors related to instructional effectiveness, implications of instructor expressiveness for improving instruction, strengthening critical thinking, evaluating teaching, moving from research to practice, and future directions for research and its application. C, CT, EI, FR, U

84. Dressell, Paul L. (1976). *Handbook of academic evaluation.* San Francisco: Jossey-Bass. 518 pp.

This volume's 18 chapters are grouped in three parts: basic considerations, evaluation of student experience and educational progress, and evaluation of programs and personnel. An epilogue discusses costs, decisions, and politics. Each chapter includes a summary and brief bibliographic note. A 46-page bibliography is included. A, AD, AY, BI, C, CE, CU, E, EV, FA, G, GD, GN, GR, IA, OA, PA, SS, SW, TH

85. DuBois, Henry J. (1988, July). Assessment centers for the development of academic libraries: A foot in the door. *Journal of Academic Librarianship, 14*(3), 154-160.

Assessment centers can be used to enhance the selection, professional development, and promotion of librarians. This article describes the benefits of a center method, users of the center, unionization and assessment for development, financial implications of centers, and strategies for establishment and planning of a center. AO, CA

86. Dunbar, Stephen B. (1991). *On the development of a national assessment of college student learning: Measurement policy and practice in perspective.* Iowa City, IA: University of Iowa. (ERIC Document Reproduction Service No. ED 340 755)

This paper was commissioned by the U.S. Department of Education as background for a study design workshop for a national assessment of college student learning held in November 1991. The author reviews problems of measurement in a national assessment of college student learning, including the consequences and content of measurement and the development of standards. He suggests a research plan for collecting information on the learning of college students. Three commentaries on this report are included. (ERIC) BI, EV, NT, OA, PR

87. Dunbar, Stephen B. (1993). Development of a national assessment of college student learning: Measurement policy and practice in perspective. *Journal of General Education, 42*(2), 83-104.

The author discusses policy issues and technical difficulties involved in developing a national assessment of college student learning in support of National Education Goal 5 (now 6): goals to be achieved, scales to be used, ways to measure knowledge and skills, and measurement challenges (consequences, content to be measured, standards, and values). The author recommends a program of research to address new challenges of national assessment and provides information to support national assessment. AY, EV, FR, G, I, MO, NT, OA, PR, S, TC

88. Edgerton, Russell. (1990, September/October). Assessment at half time. *Change, 22*(5), 4-5.

The president of AAHE assesses the state of assessment four years into the national assessment movement and suggests five principles that should inform higher education's response to pressure to assess. OA

89. Edgerton, Russ. (1991, December). National standards are coming! . . . National standards are coming! *AAHE Bulletin, 44*(4), 8-12.

The author reviews the pressure for standards for what graduates should know and be able to do for K-12 schools, progress in developing these standards, and the role higher education should play in strengthening the schools and in achieving the National Education Goals. He calls for higher educational standards for colleges and universities. OA, SS

90. Edgerton, Russell, Hutchings, Patricia, & Quinlan, Kathleen. (1991). *The teaching portfolio: Capturing the scholarship in teaching.* Washington, DC: American Association for Higher Education Teaching Initiative. 65 pp.

This monograph sets forward the case for using teaching portfolios, advances a point of view about the important issues of design, and offers a range of illustrations of what portfolio entries might look like. FA, PT, SF

91. Education Commission of the States. (1991). *Assessing college outcomes: What state leaders need to know.* Denver, CO: Author. 24 pp.

This booklet answers basic questions of state policymakers about assessing outcomes in higher education and characteristics of effective state policy. AY, OA, SW

92. *Education pilot criteria.* (1995). Gaithersburg, MD: United States Department of Commerce Technology Administration, National Institute of Standards and Technology. 41 pp.

This booklet describes the Education Pilot Criteria for the Malcolm Baldrige National Quality Award Program. The seven categories of criteria include Leadership, Information and Analysis, Strategic and Operational Planning, Human Resource Development and Management, Educational and Business Process Management, School Performance Results, and Student Focus and Student and Stakeholder Satisfaction. Also included are eligibility categories and restrictions, fees, and other information. AD, CQ, CR, D, GN, IN, IR, IW, MG, MT, OA, PA, PE, PI, SC, U

93. Edwards, Dee, & Williams, David. (1985). An experiment in self-monitoring amongst tutors at the Open University: The Mr Dummy Scheme. *British Journal of Educational Technology, 16*(1), 21-33.

The authors, faculty members at the British Open University, describe in detail the assessment system used by the OU to monitor learning in its far-flung, non-resident,

and part-time student body. They describe an experiment to examine the degree of inter-rater reliability in assessments of student writing and its effects on students' grades. EV, EX, I, IT, OA, MT, PA, PR, TC, TH, TR, W

94. Ehrmann, Stephen C. (1995). Local assessment of educational strategies that use computing, video, and telecommunications. In Thomas A. Angelo & Monica M. Manning (Eds.), *Improving learning: Forging better connections between assessment, quality & accreditation. Commissioned Papers for the 10th Annual Conference on Assessment & Quality.* Washington, DC: American Association for Higher Education.

This paper describes activities and methods developed by the Flashlight Project to develop means of assessing and evaluating the use of technology in colleges and universities. TE

95. Elliot, Norbert, Plata, Maximino, & Zelhart, Paul. (1990). *A program development handbook for the holistic assessment of writing.* Lanham, MD: University Press of America. 142 pp.

This comprehensive handbook for the holistic assessment of writing includes writing assessment and its diverse purposes; developing programs of writing assessment; a history of writing assessment in twentieth century America; measuring levels of literacy; developing prompts; administering assessment; selecting sample training papers; administering reading of papers; collecting, analyzing and reporting data; junior-level basic writing courses; and summary comments. BI, BS, C, H, HP, I, OA, TC, TN, W

96. English, Fenwick W. (1987). *Curriculum management for schools, colleges, business.* Springfield, IL: Charles C Thomas. 306 pp.

Although this book is focused largely at the K-12 level, the author contributes detailed information about systematic thinking regarding the college curriculum. Assessment is central in chapters on curricular alignment, mapping (ascertaining the actual versus the intended curriculum), auditing, and evaluation. AU, CA, H, PA, U

97. Erwin, T. Dary. (1991). *Assessing student learning and development: A guide to the principles, goals, and methods of determining college outcomes.* San Francisco: Jossey-Bass. 208 pp.

This book details the importance of student outcomes assessment by higher education faculty, student affairs professionals, and administrators. After background information and examples of institutional assessment programs around the country come a series of chapters on assessment steps, including establishing objectives, selecting methods, designing new methods, collecting and maintaining information (especially quantitative), analyzing the information and drawing conclusions, and reporting and using assessment information. The conclusion focuses on implementation of assessment programs and the future of assessment in higher education. Three appendices include proficiency guidelines for rating student foreign language speaking ability, an alumni questionnaire, and a student involvement survey. A, CA, ET, G, H, I, IS, IW, MT, O, OA, PP, SN, SU, TC, TH, U

98. Erwin, T. Dary. (1996). Assessment, evaluation, and research. In S. R. Komives & D. B. Woodard (Eds.), *Student services: A handbook for the profession* (3rd ed., pp. 415-432). San Francisco: Jossey-Bass.

This chapter provides a broad overview of assessment, evaluation, and research, including a discussion of the definitions of and distinctions among these three concepts, ways to decide the focus and best methodology for assessment, and ways to use and report resulting information. GN, MT, SN, U

99. Erwin, T. Dary. (1993). Outcomes assessment. In M. J. Barr (Ed.), *The handbook of student affairs administration* (pp. 230-241). San Francisco: Jossey-Bass.

After distinguishing among research, assessment, and evaluation, the author discusses assessment on college campuses as a response to calls for accountability. Strategies for beginning outcome assessment include defining the purpose or objective for assessment, choosing an instrument for measurement, collecting the data or information, and using the assessment information for decision making or change. CH, MT, OA, SN, TC, U

100. Evans, Nancy J. (1985). Needs assessment methodology: A comparison of results. *Journal of College Student Personnel, 26*, 107-114.

Three research questions were posed to determine the relative value of different methods of needs assessment: theory-based, objective instruments; empirically derived objective instruments; a semi-structured interview; and a combination of the theory-based, semi-structured interview and a general, semi-structured interview. Different methods produced similar general information but different concerns and degree of specificity. The clearest and most comprehensive needs assessment resulted from the theory-based questionnaire. Also included are other considerations about needs assessments of students. IS, MT, NA, SN

101. Ewell, Peter T. (1984). *The self-regarding institution: Information for excellence.* Boulder, CO: National Center for Higher Education Management Systems. 103 pp.

One of the NCHEMS Executive Overview Series, this book introduces readers to educational excellence as a change concept, outcomes, the attributes of successful institutional assessment programs, and institutional assessment and self-renewal. One book section describes attributes, includes examples of vigorous assessment programs from several institutions, discusses common objections to assessment, and identifies four themes of "information for excellence" programs. The book includes a typology of outcome dimensions. CO, EX, O, OA, SR, TA, TH

102. Ewell, Peter T. (Ed.). (1985). *Assessing educational outcomes.* New Directions for Institutional Research, No. 47. San Francisco: Jossey-Bass. 128 pp.

The book contains chapters on problems in research on student outcomes and on some well-known models of collegiate outcome assessment in the mid-1980s: the University of Tennessee-Knoxville, Northeast Missouri State University (now Truman State University), and Alverno College. Other chapters discuss developing and using a longitudinal outcome data bank, designing follow-up studies of former students, increasing the use of outcome information, and summary implications. An appendix contains sources of information on student outcomes and their assessment. CO, DB, EX, LS, MT, OA, PG, PR, RU, SU, TH, U

103. Ewell, Peter T. (1985, November/December). Assessment: What's it all about? *Change, 16*(8), 32-36.

The author reviews early assessment efforts, the pressures producing them, and student abilities being assessed. AY, OA, SW

104. Ewell, Peter T. (1987). *Assessment, accountability, and improvement: Managing the contradiction.* Washington, DC: AAHE Assessment Forum. 20 pp.

The author provides a review of assessment's recent history, an overview of the reasons for interest in accountability, and an extended discussion of assessment for accountability versus improvement: deciding what and how to assess, organizing the effort, and communicating the results. A discussion of three principles for responding to assessment mandates is followed by a bibliography. AR, AY, HP, OA, SW

105. Ewell, Peter T. (1987, January/February). Assessment: Where are we? *Change, 19*(1), 23-28.

The author reviews the spread of state outcome assessment initiatives, conferences, granting agency activity, and institutional efforts in the United States. AY, OA, SW

106. Ewell, Peter T. (Ed.). (1989). *Enhancing information use in decision making.* New Directions for Institutional Research, No. 64. San Francisco: Jossey-Bass. 95 pp.

Seven chapters by the editor and other authors discuss the role of information in institutions of higher education in the formation of policy, planning, and decision making. Chapters deal with the specific uses of information, barriers to using information and the differences among organizations, psychological principles that can enhance the communication and use of information, understanding and using research on group processes to improve decision making, improving written institutional research reports to enhance the credibility and acceptance of the research, and using electronic media to improve problem solving and dissemination of the results of research. A final chapter by the editor summarizes the book by asking four basic questions that can organize thinking about research and reports. DB, EV, IR, MT, PL, SC, T

107. Ewell, Peter T. (1991). To capture the ineffable: New forms of assessment in higher education. In Gerald Grant (Ed.), *Review of research in education* (Vol. 17, pp. 75-125). San Francisco: Jossey-Bass.

This article reviews the complex historical background of the modern assessment movement, describes Terenzini's (1989) Taxonomy of Assessment Activities in Higher Education and its methodological imperatives, and discusses three trends in assessment: development of special-purpose instruments to replace off-the-shelf tests; a shift from understanding student development as "an additive 'production process'" to recognizing complex, nonlinear development; and assessment through naturalistic methods; and actual performance of tasks rather than responses to test items. Specific topics are new tests for general education, standardized testing, generic instruments, longitudinal designs, holistic and hierarchical models; of learning, curriculum-embedded assessment, classroom research that integrates assessment and instruction, emerging issues in naturalistic assessment, and general emerging issues and future research directions. A substantial bibliography completes the article. AY, BI, C, EV, FR, GE, GN, HP, IS, M, OA, SU, SW, TA, TH, U

108. Ewell, Peter T. (1991, November/December). Back to the future: Assessment and public accountability. *Change, 23*(6), 12-17.

This article reviews state and national efforts to assess college student outcomes. The author notes "a new note of insistence is pervading public rhetoric concerning outcomes and accountability" (p. 12). He describes issues, problems, and patterns among these efforts and an emerging agenda for national and state interest in outcome assessment. AY, NT, OA, SW

109. Ewell, Peter T. (1992). Outcomes assessment, institutional effectiveness, and accreditation: A conceptual exploration. In *Accreditation, assessment and institutional effectiveness: Resource papers for the COPA Task Force on Institutional Effectiveness* (pp. 1-17). Washington, DC: Council on Postsecondary Accreditation.

This article introduces a typology of terms concerning institutional outcomes, effectiveness, and accreditation and then discusses these three concepts in detail. The author introduces six operational dilemmas and suggests principles for future policy. AR, IE, IN, IW, OA, SD, TA, TH

110. Ewell, Peter T. (1994). *A preliminary study of the feasibility and utility for national policy of instructional "good practice" indicators in undergraduate education* (NCES 94-437). Washington, DC: U.S. Department of Education, Office of Educational Research and Improvement, National Center for Education Statistics. 55 pp.

This report describes how indirect measures can provide valuable information in support of national higher education policy. Included are a review of the literature on "good practice," indicators of good educational processes, and available data-gathering instruments and methods. AD, AY, BI, CA, EI, GE, IN, IS, IW, NT, PA, PE, SU, TA, TH, TN, U

111. Ewell, Peter T. (1994). The assessment movement: Implications for teaching and learning. In Terry O'Banion & Associates (Eds.), *Teaching and learning in the community college* (pp. 73-96). Washington, DC: American Association of Community Colleges.

The author emphasizes assessing student outcomes in the community college and using assessment to improve professional practice within the institution. He reviews the history of assessment in the United States and describes specific principles of effective assessment and use of assessment results to improve teaching and learning. He emphasizes the importance of formulating clear outcome goals and incorporating assessment within a more comprehensive quality-improvement framework such as that of Continuous Quality Improvement (Total Quality Management). CC, CQ, G, HP, OA, S, TH, U

112. Ewell, Peter T. (1994, November/December). A matter of integrity: Accountability and the future of self-regulation. *Change, 26*(6), 24-29.

The author discusses the current disarray of traditional self-regulatory accreditation of higher education and higher education's inadequate response to society's changes and current educational needs. He describes changes in the environment for higher education, discusses attitudes in a frontier myth held within colleges and universities, holds out a new view of higher education's responsibility to society, and describes characteristics of effective self-regulation. AY, IW

113. Ewell, Peter T. (in press). Accountability and assessment: Recycling quality and performance data. In Marvin W. Peterson, David D. Dill, Lisa A. Mets, & Associates (Eds.), *Planning and management for a changing environment: A handbook on redesigning post-secondary institution.* San Francisco: Jossey-Bass.

This chapter examines the evolution of assessment during the late 1980s and early 1990s from "end-point checking on goal-achievement" to "continuous low-level monitoring of instructional processes and their interconnections." The author reviews current practice in assessment and suggests future trends related to accountability to external stakeholders, planning and decision making, and instruction. Assessment will be a key component of self-paced, multimedia modules and asynchronous, distance education. Assessments in the next century "must not only examine 'value added' but must themselves add value. And only the approaches that meet this condition can and should be maintained." The author offers several recommendations to academic administrators for successful assessment with demands for greater productivity and the impact of technology. AY, GN, HP, IW, PL, S

114. Ewell, Peter T., & Boyer, Carol M. (1988, July/August). Acting out state-mandated assessment: Evidence from five states. *Change, 20*(4), 40-47.

This is a summary of a study of outcome assessment efforts in Colorado, Missouri, New Jersey, South Dakota, and Virginia based on visits to the states and interviews with people involved in these programs. (Also see Boyer, Ewell, Finney, and Mingle, 1987.) AY, OA, SW

115. Ewell, Peter T., & Jones, Dennis P. (1985). *The costs of assessment.* [NCHEMS Monograph No. 8]. Boulder, CO: National Center for Higher Education Management Systems. 38 pp.

This monograph discusses costs involved with implementing an assessment program. CA

116. Ewell, Peter T., & Jones, Dennis P. (1991). *Actions matter: The case for indirect measures in assessing higher education's progress on the national education goals.* Washington, DC: U.S. Department of Education. (ERIC Document Reproduction Service No. ED 340 756)

This paper was commissioned by the U.S. Department of Education as background for a study design workshop for a national assessment of college student learning held in November 1991. The author suggests a series of indirect measures of college student learning, largely process, to be used with outcome measures. Easier to develop than direct measures, indirect assessments permit fast availability of information. Strengths and weaknesses of these methods are followed by comments from three reviewers. (ERIC) BI, MT, NT, OA, PA, PR

117. Ewell, Peter T., & Lisensky, Robert P. (1988). *Assessing institutional effectiveness: Redirecting the self-study process.* Washington, DC: Consortium for the Advancement of Private Higher Education. 110 pp.

This account of efforts of 10 small liberal arts colleges to assess their outcomes discusses institutional effectiveness as a concept; institutional goals; distinctiveness in curriculum, student populations represented, and values; use of data already available on campus; liberal education; institutionalization of information; and summary recommendations for self-study and assessment. The book includes four appendices of materials from the project: an analytical table of contents for a self-study, an inventory of existing assessment information, an outline format for departmental data assembly, and an alumni questionnaire. CU, EX, G, H, IS, LA, MT, O, OA, PG, SC, SS, TA, TH

118. Facione, Peter A. (1990). *Critical thinking: A statement of expert consensus for the purposes of educational assessment and instruction.* 95 pp. (ERIC Document Reproduction Service No. ED 315 423)

This report, conducted by the Committee on Pre-College Philosophy of the American Philosophical Association, describes a two-year study of critical thinking using an iterative Delphi technique by a panel of 46 experts on thinking, about half philosophers and half social scientists, educators, and natural scientists. The report describes characteristics of critical thinkers, skills and dispositions of critical thinking, recommendations on critical thinking instruction and assessment, research methodology used, and members of the research panel. Three appendices describe commercially available critical thinking tools, a bibliography that emphasizes assessment, and research correspondence from the project. BI, CD, CT, MT, OA, U

119. Farmer, Daniel W. (1988). *Enhancing student learning: Emphasizing essential competencies in academic programs.* Wilkes Barre, PA: King's College. 281 pp.

This book describes the Outcomes-Oriented Curriculum and Course-Embedded Assessment Model used at King's College. Written by the dean of the College, the book discusses planning for excellence and change and preparing the faculty to meet the challenge of curricular change. An Integrated Plan for Learning includes conceptualizing the curriculum; transferable skills in liberal learning; knowledge, traditional disciplines, and interdisciplinary perspectives; responsible believing and acting; linking assessment and learning; the purpose of assessment; a course-embedded assessment model; and assessment strategies. Faculty essays describe the King's College four-year Competency Growth Plan concept, guidelines for writing critical and argumentative essays, critical thinking in the disciplines, linking the library with pedagogy and curriculum, making learning objectives explicit, sophomore-junior diagnostic programs, and senior-level integrated assessments. Included are many outcomes, criteria, and indicators from disciplinary major programs. Available from King's College, Wilkes Barre, PA 18711.
A, C, CR, DI, EX, GE, IN, M, O, OA, TH, U

120. Feinberg, Lawrence. (1990, Fall). Multiple-choice and its critics: Are the "alternatives" any better? *College Board Review* No. 17, 12-17, 30.

The author compares the strengths and weaknesses of multiple-choice tests and their authentic or performance-based alternatives and shows that difficulties are inherent in all forms of test design. EV, PR, PS

121. Fenske, Robert H. (Ed.). (1978). *Using goals in research and planning.* New Directions for Institutional Research, No. 19. San Francisco: Jossey-Bass. 90 pp.

Six chapters by various authors address the use of goals in colleges and universities. Discussions focus on the development of criteria for goals, assessment of goals, use of the ETS Institutional Goals Inventory, and use of goals at the University of Toledo and North Carolina Central University. A final chapter by the editor provides a synthesis and suggests implications for research. CR, EX, FR, IR, IS, IW, MS, MT, OA, PI, PR, TH

122. Fetterman, David M. (Ed.). (1991). *Using qualitative methods in institutional research.* New Directions for Institutional Research, No. 72. San Francisco: Jossey-Bass. 88 pp.

Six chapters by various authors discuss the value of qualitative approaches for studying issues in higher education. Individual chapters describe ethnographic interviews,

auditing, student portfolios in the fine arts, case studies of graduate student socialization, and political and logistical issues when integrating qualitative and quantitative assessments of the quality of academic life. A final chapter by the editor describes resources for qualitative research. AU, DI, GD, I, IR, OA, P

123. Fitt, David X., & Heverly, Maryann. (1994). Classroom assessment of student competencies. *Assessment & Evaluation in Higher Education, 19*(3), 215-224.

This article describes a study examining a method of exploring the content of a course by comparing students' ratings of their understanding of specific concepts or procedures on entry and at the end of a course against teachers' ratings of the amount of coverage of the competency in the course. Pre- and post-test results may be substituted for student judgment, and the method described can help specification of student competencies, assessment of mastery, faculty interaction, student involvement in assessment, and development of a climate of self-assessment and continuous quality improvement, and provide assistance to adjunct faculty. C, CQ, GD, I, IA, MT, OA, PA, SA, TH, U

124. Folger, John K., & Harris, John W. (1989). *Assessment in accreditation.* [Atlanta, GA: Southern Association of Schools and Colleges.] 140 pp.

This introduction to assessment in the context of accreditation includes definitions of assessment, accreditation, and accountability; elements of institutional effectiveness; the visiting committee; and developing an assessment program. Appendices include evaluating a statement of purpose; criterion measures (differences between research on instruction and research for selection of people); a condensed version of a University of Tennessee-Knoxville bibliography of assessment instruments; and case studies from James Madison University, St. Petersburg Junior College, and Trinity University. Available from the Southern Association of Colleges and Schools (SACS).
AR, AY, BI, CC, EX, MS, OA, SC, SM, TH

125. Fong, Bobby. (1987, June 14-17). *The external examiner approach to assessment.* Paper presented at the Second AAHE National Conference on Assessment in Higher Education, Denver, CO. 21 pp.

The author reviews using external examiners to assess student outcomes in higher education, contrasts the British and American situations, and suggests that the British model of external examiners is inappropriate for this country. He then shows how external examiners might be used in the United States, discusses issues of validity and reliability, and provides examples of the use of external examiners in U.S. colleges and universities. BI, EE, HP, IN, OA, TC

126. Fong, Bobby. (1988). Assessing the departmental major. In James H. McMillan (Ed.), *Assessing students' learning.* New Directions for Teaching and Learning, No. 34 (pp. 71-83). San Francisco: Jossey-Bass.

The author discusses the objectives, purposes, and effects of assessment and expectations and the faculty culture of departments, the strengths and weaknesses of both commercially designed instruments and locally developed assessments of various sorts, and the use of external examiners. CA, IS, M, OA

127. Forrest, Aubrey, & Associates. (1990). *Time will tell: Portfolio-assisted assessment of general education.* Washington, DC: American Association for Higher Education Assessment Forum. 30 pp.

Prepared by a 13-person AAHE faculty Study Group on Portfolio Assessment, this brief account gives the rationale for portfolio assessment and describes how to establish an institutional portfolio program. The use of portfolios in 16 institutions is described, together with addresses and telephone numbers of people to contact at these institutions. EX, GE, OA, P

128. Gaither, Gerald H. (Ed.). (1995). *Assessing performance in an age of accountability: Case studies.* New Directions for Higher Education, No. 91. San Francisco: Jossey-Bass. 107 pp.

Eight authors and the editor review the current use of performance indicators to appraise public institutions of higher education. Nine chapters provide an overview of policy and practice in an international movement to use performance indicators; a ten-state study of similarities and differences in state assessment efforts; detailed studies of the State University of New York, University of Wisconsin, University of Maryland, and Texas A&M University Systems, and the University of Montana, the Arkansas higher education system, and the State of Missouri. The editor establishes themes and provides resources for further study. AY, IA, OA, PI, SW

129. Gaither, Gerald, Nedwek, Brian P., & Neal, John E. (1994). *Measuring up: The promises and pitfalls of performance indicators in higher education* (ASHE-ERIC Higher Education Report No.5). Washington, DC: George Washington University Graduate School of Education and Human Development. 148 pp.

This research review introduces the current status of institutional performance indicators and describes societal forces that interest policymakers in indicators. Sets of indi-

cators from institutions and organizations are described as well as a list of "Top Ten 'Core' Indicators." One chapter describes the use of performance indicators in other nations, and a final chapter describes short-term future trends and impediments to future development. AY, BI, EX, IN, IW, MG, OA, PI, PR, SC

130. Gardiner, Lion F. (1989). *Planning for assessment: Mission statements, goals, and objectives.* Trenton, NJ: New Jersey Department of Higher Education. 256 pp.

Prepared to assist faculty members, administrators, and others involved in a statewide outcome assessment effort, this handbook draws together useful information from various professional literatures. Three chapters introduce the organizational context of planning and assessment, concepts of strategic and operational planning, and assessment and evaluation in higher education. Other chapters describe the mission review process and departmental, programmatic, and institutional mission statements; understanding, developing, reviewing, and writing effective goals and objectives; linking goals and objectives to assessment and evaluation; and useful resources. Included are an annotated bibliography and 17 appendices; conceptual tools for working with outcomes; taxonomies of student development outcomes; sample institutional mission statements and outcome statements; and goal inventories. Available from the author: 335 Greenwich Street, 14B, New York, New York 10013-3325. BI, G, H, MS, O, OA, OP, SC, SD, SP, SS, SW, TA, TB, TH

131. Gardiner, Lion F. (1994). *Redesigning higher education: Producing dramatic gains in student learning.* (ASHE-ERIC Higher Education Report No. 7). Washington, DC: George Washington University, Graduate School of Education and Human Development. 225 pp.

Using almost 700 sources, this review and synthesis of research enumerates key competencies identified by leaders in business, government, and education as essential for college graduates' personal and society's democratic and economic success, and the courses and conditions for development of these essential abilities. Several chapters summarize research about these conditions on campus in curriculum, instruction, academic advising, and campus climate. Additional chapters address the ability of today's students to learn; describe seven key recommendations of researchers about change in higher education; and identify key roles of leadership, skilled management, and professional development in producing high-quality educational results. A final chapter lays out a vision for community and caring on campus and potential for a powerful impact of colleges and universities on society. A, AA, AD, AY, BI, C, CD, CQ, CT, CU, D, DV, EI, ET, FA, FD, G, GE, GR, I, IN, IS, LS, MG, MS, OA, PA, PI, PR, RR, S, SC, TH, U

132. Gose, Kenneth F., & Thrash, Patricia A. (1991). Assessing student academic achievement. *NCA Quarterly, 66*(2), 387-488.

This issue of the NCA quarterly journal is a collection of papers on outcome assessment, several written by experienced practitioners at various institutions. Topics include the NCA Statement on Assessment and Student Academic Achievement; accreditation and assessment; designing an assessment program to meet accreditation criteria; purposes, issues, and assessment approaches in evaluation processes; deciding between commercial and locally developed instruments; and faculty participation. Part III includes case studies of assessment activities in four different institutions. AR, AY, EX, OA

133. Gray, Peter J. (Ed.). (1989). *Achieving assessment goals using evaluation techniques.* New Directions for Higher Education, No. 67. San Francisco: Jossey-Bass. 124 pp.

Knowledge gleaned from the established field of evaluation is applied to newer assessment efforts. Included are discussions of good practice, the effects of critical organizational factors on assessment practices, five guidelines, assessment as a source of data for evaluation, the need to define assessment broadly, and a synthesis and suggested future directions. EX, FR, GN, IW, OA, RU, SC, SR, TH

134. Gray, Peter J., & Banta, Trudy W. (Eds.). (in press). *Assessment revisited: Signs of progress and problems.* New Directions for Higher Education. San Francisco: Jossey-Bass.

This collection of seven chapters by 10 different authors takes stock of two decades of outcome assessment in the United States by asking whether this activity has made a difference for student learning. The book concludes that the enormous amount of assessment activity across the country has yielded relatively slight benefits to student learning, increases in institutional productivity, or other good effects. An introductory chapter examines characteristics of leadership and planned change to ease the successful use of assessment, five chapters present case studies from various institutional sectors, and a final chapter examines generalizations about successful assessment and principles to guide future assessment. CC, CH, FR, PR, RU, SR

135. Greenwood, Addison. (1993). *National assessment of college student learning: Getting started* (NCES 93-116). Washington, DC: U.S. Department of Education, Office of Educational Research and Improvement. 182 pp.

This report provides background information for and identifies issues, problems, and tasks to be considered by a second study workshop of assessment experts, held in November 1992, to lay a foundation for the design of a national assessment of college student learning. The report summarizes 15 background papers prepared for the first workshop, held in November 1991, reviewers' comments, and the proceedings of the first workshop (see also Corallo, 1992). AY, CD, CE, CT, FR, IN, IS, NT, OA, OS, PG, PR, S, SW, TC, TH, U

136. Greenwood, Addison (Ed.). (1994). *The national assessment of college student learning: Identification of the skills to be taught, learned, and assessed* (NCES 94-286). Washington, DC: U.S. Department of Education, Office of Educational Research and Improvement, National Center for Education Statistics. 313 pp.

This is a report on a second workshop of assessment experts to prepare for a national assessment of college student learning, held in November 1992. Sections by various authors address skills for citizenship, critical thinking, problem-solving, speaking and listening, and reading and writing. Included are specific competencies, means of assessing these competencies, and participant comments. AY, BI, CD, CE, CT, G, GE, H, IN, IS, MT, NT, OA, OS, PG, PR, TC, TH, W

137. Gruppen, Larry D., Wisdom, Kimberlydawn, Anderson, David S., & Woolliscroft, James O. (1993). Assessing the consistency and educational benefits of students' clinical experiences during an ambulatory care internal medicine rotation. *Academic Medicine, 68*(9), 674-680.

The authors studied the experiences of 43 students in the M. D. program at the University of Michigan Medical School during a one-month clinical rotation. They found "numerous and potentially worrisome gaps" (p. 674) in the students' exposure to various typical patient problems. The authors discuss the origins of variability of experience in clinical training and suggest these clinical education problems are very likely typical of other areas in medicine. This study provides a model for assessing the quality of clinical experience outside of medicine as well. CL, DI, EI, EX, GD, MT, PA, SI

138. Halasa, Ofelia. (1977). The interdependency of product and process assessment in educational evaluation. *Educational Technology, 17,* 55-57.

This article shows the importance of assessing not only outcomes but also the processes that produce them. OA, PA, TH

139. Halpern, Diane F. (Ed.). (1987). *Student outcomes assessment: What institutions stand to gain.* New Directions for Higher Education, No. 59. San Francisco: Jossey-Bass. 116 pp.

Topics in chapters in this book include an introduction to and overview of outcome assessment, establishing a campus-based assessment program, a state university system perspective and reviews of outcome assessment in the California State Master Plan, performance funding in Tennessee, assessment as a means of increasing learning at Northeast Missouri State University (now Truman State University), assessing general education at Trenton State College (now College of New Jersey), mandated CLAST testing in Florida, a historical perspective on higher education expansion and assessment, the concept of value added and assessment, and a final chapter of recommendations and caveats. AY, EX, HP, OA, SR, SW, TH, VA

140. Hanna, Gerald S., & Cashin, William E. (1987, September). *Matching instructional objectives, subject matter, tests, and score interpretations* (IDEA Paper No. 18). Manhattan, KS: Kansas State University, Center for Faculty Evaluation and Development. 6 pp.

This leaflet integrates learning objectives, course content, assessments, and interpretation of scores. Included are discussions of types of instruction, instructional objectives, tests, types of test interpretations, and test scores. To obtain copies call (800) 255-2757. C, EV, I, O, OA, TH

141. Hanna, Gerald S., & Cashin, William E. (1988, January). *Improving college grading* (IDEA Paper No. 19). Manhattan, KS: Kansas State University, Center for Faculty Evaluation and Development. 6 pp.

This leaflet describes and critiques two prototypic grading systems: percentage and class-curve. The authors provide criteria for grading systems and describe a system for anchoring to ensure equitable determination of grades, together with detailed examples. To obtain copies call (800) 255-2757. GR

142. Hanson, Gary R. (Ed.). (1982). *Measuring student development.* New Directions for Student Services, No. 20. San Francisco: Jossey-Bass. 124 pp.

Five chapters by various authors provide a rationale for assessing student development, describe the problem of expecting complex decision making too early in students' social-cognitive development, integrate disparate research traditions and models of college student development, describe difficulties and make suggestions for the assessment of student change, describe existing assessment methods, and provide a case study in student development assessment programming at University of Texas-Austin. The editor concludes with additional resources. A, BI, EX, FR, HP, I, IS, MT, OA, RU, SN, SU, TC, TH

143. Hanson, Gary R. (1989). *The assessment of student development outcomes: A review and critique of assessment instruments.* Trenton, NJ: New Jersey Department of Higher Education. 156 pp.

This monograph reviews instruments that purport to assess student development in college. Included are a discussion of critical issues, ways to choose instruments, and descriptions and critiques of instruments that claim to assess career, cognitive, moral, and personal development. This review is a companion to Kuh, Krehbiel, and McKay, 1988. A, BI, CD, IA, IS, LN, MT, OA, SU, TC

144. Hanson, Gary, & Huston, Christine. (1995). Academic advising and assessment. In Alice G. Reinarz & Eric R. White (Eds.), *Teaching through academic advising: A faculty perspective.* New Directions for Teaching and Learning, No. 62 (pp. 87-96). San Francisco: Jossey-Bass.

This article describes ways in which advisors can use a variety of assessment information profitably to understand their students and improve the quality of their work. AA, U

145. Harrow, Alicia J. (1972). *A taxonomy of the psychomotor domain: A guide for developing behavioral objectives.* New York: Longman. 190 pp.

This book describes the psychomotor domain of student learning and development, shows the importance of psychomotor behaviors, and discusses a rationale for and problems in classifying these behaviors. The author describes previous theories of and models for classifying movement. Most of the book is devoted to describing a taxonomy of movement behavior, writing instructional objectives in the psychomotor domain, and reviewing the literature. Examples of objectives and assessment items are included. (Also see Bloom, 1956, and Krathwohl et al., 1964, for taxonomies in the cognitive and affective domains respectively.) BI, C, G, H, HP, I, MT, O, OA, PR, TA, TH, U

146. Hogan, Thomas P. (1992). Methods for outcomes assessment related to institutional accreditation. In *Accreditation, assessment and institutional effectiveness: Resource papers for the COPA Task Force on Institutional Effectiveness* (pp. 37-55). Washington, DC: Council on Postsecondary Accreditation.

This article reviews key issues in linking assessment to accreditation: value added, useful versus perfect assessment, program effectiveness versus institutional effectiveness, the importance of goals, methods for assessing and selecting outcomes, institutional records, and the institutional assessment plan. AR, G, GE, GN, IE, IS, IW, MT, TH, VA

147. Hoyt, Donald P. (1965). *The relationship between college grades and adult achievement: A review of the literature.* Iowa City, IA: American College Testing Program. 57 pp.

This classic study reviews the validity of college grades for predicting success later in life as revealed in 46 research studies. Eight categories are examined: business, teaching, engineering, scientific research, miscellaneous occupations, studies of eminence, and non-vocational accomplishment. The author concludes that "present evidence strongly suggests that college grades bear little or no relationship to any measures of adult accomplishment" (p. i). GR, RR

148. Huebner, Lois A., & Lawson. Jane M. (1990). Understanding and assessing college environments. In D. G. Creamer (Ed.), *College student development: Theory and practice for the 1990s* (pp.127-151). Alexandria, VA: American College Personnel Association.

Lewin's paradigm of environmental fit, behavior as a function of the person and the environment, is the underlying theory of this discussion of environmental assessment. The authors discuss the components of interaction contributing to the quality and diversity of a student's unique educational experience: students, faculty, and the college environment. Six environmental constructs which influence students' development and performance include heterogeneity/homogeneity, support-challenge balance, social support, social climate, the physical environment, and person-environment congruence. For each of the constructs, definitions are given, findings are described, and issues in measurement are discussed. CM, SN, SU

149. Hughes, I. E., & Large, B. J. (1993). Staff and peer-group assessment of oral communication skills. *Studies in Higher Education, 18*(3), 379-385.

The authors studied staff and peer-group assessment of the oral communication skills of 44 pharmacology students at the University of Leeds. The study showed a strong correlation (0.83, p < 0.001) between peer-group and faculty ratings of student communication skills and a poor correlation (0.23, p > 0.1) between students' evaluations of peers and their own communication skills, which "strongly suggests that these students can make a reasoned assessment independent of their own level of skill and should therefore be in a position to assess their own performance" (p. 383). Bottom quartile students' ratings of peers did not

differ significantly from those of top quartile students (Student's t-test, p = 0.13), suggesting that poorer students are as rigorous evaluators as better students. CM, I, MT, OA, PA, PV, SA

150. Huot, Brian. (1990, May). Reliability, validity, and holistic scoring: What we know and what we need to know. *College Composition and Communication, 41*(2), 201-213.

The author addresses the validity and reliability of holistic scoring, a standard means of directly assessing the quality of written text. He maintains that the validity of holistic scoring has been slighted in the interest of ensuring inter-rater reliability and that little research has addressed either "its theoretical soundness [or] a number of serious objections that have been raised about it" (p. 201). He discusses the issues involved in the validity and reliability of holistic scoring, reviews the literature, and calls for significant research to clarify the validity of holistic scoring. DI, EV, FR, I, MT, PA, PR, RB, TC, W

151. Hutchings, Pat. (1996). *Making teaching community property: A menu for peer collaboration and peer review.* Washington, DC: American Association for Higher Education Teaching Initiative. 115 pp.

This book suggests that teaching should be seen as scholarly, intellectual work that can and should be subjected to peer review. Each chapter includes general comments as well as several faculty reports, or mini case studies, of ways that the various strategies have been implemented on campuses across the country. Examples described include teaching circles, reciprocal visits and observations, mentoring, portfolios, team teaching, collaborative inquiry, departmental collaboration, and intercampus collaboration and external review of teaching. EI, EX, FA, IC, PT, SF

152. Hutchings, Patricia A., & Marchese, Theodore J. (1990). Assessing curricular outcomes—the U.S. experience. *Higher Education Management, 2*(1), 20-26.

The authors review the American assessment movement for the international audience of this journal. They describe the purposes of assessment and the nature and growth of state assessment mandates, using New Jersey and Virginia as examples. Closing comments identify problems and concerns that will influence the future of the movement. AY, PR, SC, SW

153. Hutchings, Pat, & Marchese, Ted. (1990, September/October). Watching assessment: Questions, stories, prospects. *Change, 22*(5), 12-38.

Two senior staff members at AAHE take stock of the assessment movement after four years. They chronicle the assessment activities of various states and institutions and review AAHE's assessment conferences. HP, OA, SW

154. Hutchings, Pat, Marchese, Ted, & Wright, Barbara. (1991). *Using assessment to strengthen general education.* Washington, DC: American Association for Higher Education Assessment Forum. 42 pp.

This general overview focuses on important issues relating to integrating assessment into general education to improve the quality of student learning. Appendices contain accounts of assessment on several diverse campuses and comments from individual scholars and practitioners. CC, EX, GE, OA, RU, SC

155. Hutchings, Pat, & Reuben, Elaine. (1988/July/August). Faculty voices on assessment: Expanding the conversation. *Change, 20*(4), 48-55.

Faculty share their experiences with assessment. OA

156. Hyman, Randy E., Beeler, Karl J., & Benedict, Larry G. (1994). Outcomes assessment and student affairs: New roles and expectations. *NASPA Journal, 32,* 20-30.

Six institutions were studied through a case study approach and a 14-item questionnaire to understand uses of student outcomes assessment to improve programs and services on a college or university campus. The article includes a summary of the information collected, including descriptions of assessment efforts, uses of outcomes data, and examples of methods and instruments from each institution. The conclusion presents five key factors in successful assessment and improvement at these institutions. EX, IS, IW, OA, SN, U

157. Ingle, Henry T. (1994). *Charting campus progress in promoting ethnic diversity and cultural pluralism.* New Directions for Institutional Research, No. 81, pp. 35-50. San Francisco: Jossey-Bass.

Use of portfolio assessment as a planning and evaluation approach for institutional research in higher education is discussed. The portfolio method involves clustering seven critical performance indicators to guide campus efforts in working more realistically with issues of cultural pluralism and diversity. (ERIC) DV, MT, PI, PL

158. Jacobi, Maryann, Astin, Alexander, & Ayala, Frank, Jr. (1987). *College student outcomes assessment: A talent development perspective* (ASHE-ERIC Higher Education Report No. 7). Washington, DC: Association for the Study of Higher Education. 124 pp.

This introduction to the assessment of student development outcomes discusses the purposes and philosophy of student outcome assessment, taxonomies and typologies of outcomes, technical issues in assessing talent development, cognitive development instruments, and problems in and suggestions for assessment. An appendix provides sources

and time requirements to administer the commercially available assessment instruments discussed. BI, CD, GE, IS, OA, PR, TA, TH

159. Jacobs, Lucy Cheser, & Chase, Clinton I. (1992). *Developing and using tests effectively: A guide for faculty.* San Francisco: Jossey-Bass. 231 pp.

This handbook describes the role of classroom testing, ways to plan tests, and the technical issues of reliability and validity. Separate chapters discuss multiple-choice items; true-false, matching, and completion items; and essay examinations. The authors describe alternative assessment procedures, test administration, computer-assisted testing, item analysis, and grading. BI, C, GR, I, T, TA, TH, TS

160. Janzow, Fred, & Eison, James. (1990). Grades: Their influence on students and faculty. In Marilla D. Svinicki (Ed.), *The changing face of college teaching* (pp. 93-112). New Directions for Teaching and Learning, No. 42. San Francisco: Jossey-Bass.

The authors review research on college grades, particularly emphasizing the results of the LOGO (learning-oriented, grade-oriented) student self-report inventory. GR, IS, RR

161. Johnson, David W., & Johnson, Roger T. (1996). *Meaningful and manageable assessment through cooperative learning.* Edina, MN: Interaction. 302 pp.

Aimed primarily toward K-12 teachers, this book contains methods for assessing, using cooperative learning groups that can be adapted for colleges and universities. Included are goal setting, standardized tests, teacher-made tests, compositions and presentations, projects, student portfolios, observing students, assessing social skills and student attitudes, interviewing students, learning logs and journals, Total Quality Learning and student management teams, teaching teams, and grading. A, BI, C, CQ, G, GR, H, I, IN, IS, MT, OA, P, RB, TH, TS, U

162. Johnstone, D. Bruce. (1995). Enhancing the productivity of learning. *Journal for Higher Education Management, 11*(1), 11-17.

A former Chancellor of the State University of New York, the author articulates 10 assumptions or propositions about changes in higher education to increase productivity and efficiency. The author describes eight specific ways to increase productivity of student learning. Useful assessment information is required to describe and monitor current conditions. This article provides a framework for discussion, planning, and action. AY, GN, IW, MG, PI, SP, U

163. Jones, Elizabeth A., & Associates. (1995). *National assessment of college student learning: Identifying college graduates' essential skills in writing, speech and listening, and critical thinking* (NCES 95-001). Washington, DC: U.S. Department of Education, Office of Educational Research and Improvement, National Center for Education Statistics. 181 pp.

This report describes a study commissioned by the U.S. Department of Education in support of a national assessment of college student learning. Using an iterative Delphi process, the researchers surveyed 600 faculty members, employers, and policy makers who evaluated skills in writing, speech communication, and critical thinking for their adequacy in their work environments. Included in the report are descriptions of the Delphi process and other aspects of the study, lists of the skills or competencies and of the participants' reactions. The conclusion shows how institutions and departments can use the inventories of abilities to improve student learning. AY, BI, CD, CT, G, GE, NT, O, OA, OS, PG, RR, SS, U

164. Jordan, Thomas E. (1989). *Measurement and evaluation in higher education: Issues and illustrations.* Philadelphia: Falmer Press. 180 pp.

The author provides a brief overview and sets the context of assessment and evaluation in American higher education. Included are evaluation of academic programs and support services, testing, a description of a study using the College Student Experiences Questionnaire, and a discussion of evaluation and change. AY, C, G, GE, GN, HP, IN, IS, MT, S, SW

165. Judd, Charles M. (1987, Fall). Combining process and outcome assessment. In Melvin M. Mark & Lance Shotland (Eds.), *Multiple methods in program evaluation.* New Directions for Program Evaluation, No. 35 (pp. 23-41). San Francisco: Jossey-Bass.

The author contends that focused attention on educational processes and process research must be combined with outcome assessment for maximal conceptual power. He discusses the procedures of process evaluation, problems with analyzing causes of outcomes, and the integration of process and outcome research. MT, PA, PE, TH

166. Kaase, Kristopher J., & Harshbarger, D. Bruce. (1993). Applying focus groups in student affairs assessment. *NASPA Journal, 30,* 284-289.

Focus groups enhance more traditional, quantitative ways of learning about students. General tips for conducting successful focus groups include information on selecting the group, recording the session, and understanding the moderator's role. Effective interpretation, understanding, and use of results can initiate change. This article introduces focus groups to student affairs professionals using focus groups for the first time. EX, MT, SN, U

167. Kaufman, Robert. (1987, October). A needs assessment primer. *Training and Development Journal, 41,* 78-83.

This 10-step guide focuses on planning and conducting a needs assessment. MT, NA

168. Kaufman, Roger, & English, Fenwick W. (1979). *Needs assessment: Concept and application.* Englewood Cliffs, NJ: Educational Technology Publications. 355 pp.

This basic handbook of needs assessment in schools describes a conceptual framework for and application of needs assessment. H, MT, NA, TA, TH

169. Kells, H. R. (1981). Some theoretical suggestions for institutional assessment. In Richard I. Miller (Ed.), *Institutional assessment for self-improvement.* New Directions for Institutional Research, No. 29 (pp. 15-26). San Francisco: Jossey-Bass.

This critique of common approaches to assessment includes principles to guide an institutional assessment effort. AY, OA

170. Kells, H. R. (1992). *Self-regulation in higher education: A multi-national perspective in collaborative systems of quality assurance and control* (Higher Education Policy Series 15). London: Jessica Kingsley. 238 pp.

This international review of self-regulation in higher education features an historical and conceptual framework of regulation; purposes and general methods of evaluation; models of regulation; processes of self-regulation, current and proposed systems in nations in Europe, Africa, the Americas, and Asia; and the future of self-regulation. Six appendices contain sources of information; modular survey instruments; excerpts from program review and institutional evaluation documents from the Netherlands, British Columbia, France, and the United Kingdom, and a WASC accreditation handbook (the United States). AR, AY, BI, D, FR, HP, IT, IS, IW, PI, PR, SL

171. Kells, H. R. (1995). *Self-study processes: A guide to self-evaluation in higher education.* Phoenix, AZ: Oryx. 194 pp.

This handbook is for researchers of higher education. Chapters detail the self-study process and include instruction, examples and cases, illustrations, and references.

Included are discussions of the management and organizational context for self-evaluation; management of quality; advice for work groups; preparing a report; self-evaluation of people, programs, and institutions; the review cycle, including external peer review, and consultant and team visits; accrediting agencies; and development of a culture of self-regulation. Four appendices contain sources of information and assistance, questions concerning 14 aspects of program review, a modular instrument for collecting data for self-evaluation, and a follow-up questionnaire for graduates. AR, EX, G, H, IS, PE, SL, U

172. Kingan, Mary E., & Alfred, Richard L. (1993). Entry assessment in community colleges: Tracking or facilitating? *Community College Review, 21*(3), 3-16.

The authors argue against using placement assessment as a device for tracking students and for using it to facilitate students' learning in college. They review the literature and give specific examples, including flow charts of assessment and provision of assistance to students, from various institutions. BS, CC, EX, IA, PC, PR, TH, U

173. Kirschenbaum, Howard, Napier, Rodney, & Simon, Sidney B. (1971). *Wad-ja-get? The grading game in American education.* New York: Hart. 315 pp.

Set in the K-12 sector, but relevant to higher education, this book explores the uses and problems of grades. It includes recommendations for change and appendices with an annotated bibliography of research on grading and descriptions of alternative grading systems. GR

174. Kloss, Robert J. (1992). Can general education be assessed? One state's positive answer. *Journal of General Education, 41,* 177-189.

The author describes the development of the New Jersey General Intellectual Skills Assessment (GIS), a component of the COEP statewide assessment effort, by a team of 18 New Jersey faculty members and ETS professionals. Described are test content (unique free-response tasks), results of the first administration of the GIS, reporting of scores, issues of student motivation, and faculty resistance to administration of the assessment. (The GIS is now known as the ETS Tasks in Critical Thinking.) CD, CT, I, IN, IS, MO, MT, OA, PR, SW, W

175. Kogan, Maurice (Ed.). (1989). *Evaluating higher education* (Higher Education Policy Series No. 6). London: Jessica Kingsley. 220 pp.

In 24 chapters various authors review assessment and evaluation in higher education internationally. Sections review approaches and techniques as well as evaluating institutions, faculty, courses, departments, and research. Representative chapters review assessment at Northeast Missouri State University (now Truman State University)

and University of Tennessee-Knoxville, internal evaluation, course evaluation, academic program review and university priorities, methods for evaluating research, and resource allocation based on evaluation of research. AR, AY, D, EI, EX, FA, IE, IT, IW, NT, PE, PI, PR, S, SW, VA

176. Krathwohl, David R., Bloom, Benjamin S., & Masia, Bertram B. (1964). *Taxonomy of educational objectives: The classification of educational goals. Handbook II: Affective domain.* White Plains, NY: Longman. 196 pp.

Second of two volumes describing the Taxonomy of Educational Objectives, this book describes the affective domain, having to do with interest, appreciation, attitudes, value, adjustment, and will. *Part I* describes the development of the Taxonomy, the need and basis for the classification of affective objectives, relationship of the affective and cognitive domains, classification of affective educational objectives and test items, and the relationship between the Taxonomy and curriculum, assessment, and research. Typical affective objectives and test items are provided. *Part II*, about half of the book, details the affective Taxonomy. Two appendices contain condensed versions of the Affective Domain and the Cognitive Domain of the Taxonomy. (Also see Bloom, 1956, for the companion volume describing the Taxonomy in the cognitive domain and Harrow, 1972, for an unrelated taxonomy in the psychomotor domain.) A, C, CU, H, I, MT, O, OA, OS, TA, TH

177. Kuh, George D. (1982). Purposes and principles of needs assessment in student affairs. *Journal of College Student Personnel, 23,* 202-209.

This article provides an overview of the what, why, and how of needs assessment. Needs assessment is approached as a "problem-focusing" activity rather than a goal generation activity. Definitions of need include democratic, discrepancy, maintenance, and incremental. Five purposes of needs assessments are considered, with advantages, disadvantages, and an illustration given for each. Six guiding principles are outlined as a framework for work of a needs assessment team. NA, PP, SN

178. Kuh, George D. (1993). Assessing campus environments. In M. J. Barr (Ed.) *The handbook of student affairs administration* (pp. 30-48). San Francisco: Jossey-Bass.

The relationship between institutional context and student learning is the foundation for assessing campus environments. Within a framework for assessing the influence of institutional properties on learning and personal development are substantive frames that focus on the "primary student-institutional points of contact where learning is likely to occur" and the interpretive frames that are used "as a filter or lens through which to analyze and understand how students' experiences influence their behavior" (p. 32). The chapter concludes with eight key issues in conducting campus audits and assessing campus climates. CG, CM, I, MS, SN

179. Kuh, George D., Krehbiel, Lee E., & MacKay, Kathleen. (1988). *Personal development and the college student experience: A review of the literature.* Trenton, NJ: New Jersey Department of Higher Education. 130 pp.

Commissioned by the New Jersey statewide assessment program, this monograph reviews student personal development in college. Included are the rationale for personal development as an important outcome of college; theoretical foundation for and empirical research on personal development in college; undergraduate experience, satisfaction, involvement, and assessable indices for personal development; and implications for assessment teams. Included are a 20-page bibliography, a 14-page annotated bibliography, a taxonomy of personal development outcomes, an assessment plan from James Madison University, a list of outcome assessment areas from Murray State University, and a description of assessment methods. This review is a companion to Hanson, 1989. A, BI, EX, O, TA

180. Lasley, Thomas J., & Haberman, Martin. (1987). How do university administrators evaluate education deans? *Journal of Teacher Education, 38*(5), 13-16.

The authors studied criteria used by vice-presidents and vice-chancellors at 66 NASULGC institutions to evaluate their education deans. AD, CR, I

181. Lawton, Richard. (1986). The role of the external examiner. *Journal of Geography in Higher Education, 10*(1), 41-51.

The author describes the British system of external examiners in higher education, focusing on the discipline of geography. In Britain and in African nations, the external examiner's role is to ensure the quality of first degrees awarded by institutions of higher education. The external examiner is responsible for ensuring the quality of courses, the following of regulations about requirements and assessments for degrees, fairness, and a check on decisions made within degree programs. The author identifies and makes suggestions for overcoming problems in the external examiner system. AR, AY, DI, EE, EI, I, IC, IT, OA, PA, PE, PR, SC, TH

182. Lenning, Oscar T. (1977). *Previous attempts to structure educational outcomes and outcome-related concepts: A compilation and review of the literature.* Boulder, CO: National Center for Higher Education Management Systems. 231 pp.

This volume gathers together almost 90 taxonomies, typologies, and lists of outcomes, based on an exhaustive search of the literature of higher education. BI, G, O, OS, TA

183. Lenth, Charles S. (1991). *The context and policy requisites of national postsecondary assessment.* Denver, CO: Education Commission of the States. (ERIC Document Reproduction Service No. ED 340 757)

This paper was commissioned by the U.S. Department of Education as background for a study design workshop for a national assessment of college student learning held in November 1991. The author reviews a number of state-level assessment programs, describes the purposes and aims of both state and national assessments and their relationship to each other, and discusses the needs for support and commitment required for a national assessment. Included are the comments of three reviewers. (ERIC) NT, OA, SW

184. Lenth, Charles S. (Ed.). (1991). *Using national data bases.* New Directions for Institutional Research, No. 69. San Francisco: Jossey-Bass. 115 pp.

Six chapters by various authors discuss how to use national data bases. Specific topics are using data to study the success of minority group students, using national data to develop a local data base, using national faculty surveys, accessing Federal data by means of the NSF CASPAR System, and using financial data. An annotated guide to data bases and statistical resources complete the book. DB, DV, NT, ST, SW

185. Lesh, Richard, & Lamon, Susan J. (Eds.). (1992). *Assessment of authentic performance in school mathematics.* Washington, DC: American Association for the Advancement of Science. 445 pp.

Sixteen detailed and specific chapters by various authors describe how to assess mathematics knowledge and skills and focus "on 'real-life' situations, 'authentic' mathematics, and 'performance' activities" (p. 3). Although directed to K-12 assessment, this book can help faculty in higher education attempting to assess mathematics learning. CD, DI, I, OA

186. Light, Richard J. (1990). *The Harvard Assessment Seminars: Exploration with students and faculty about teaching, learning, and student life.* Cambridge, MA: Harvard University Graduate School of Education. 96 pp.

This first report of the Harvard Assessment Seminars describes the background of the Seminars, five main and several minor findings, and the embedding of research and evaluation in ongoing activities. A list of participants in the Seminars is included. EI, EX, PA, PG, RU, U

187. Light, Richard J. (1992). *The Harvard Assessment Seminars: Exploration with students and faculty about teaching, learning, and student life.* Cambridge, MA: Harvard University Graduate School of Education. 89 pp.

This second report of the Harvard Assessment Seminars focuses on the "extraordinary impact of students' collegial relationships built around academic work," the impact of writing on student development, ways that advisors can help students help themselves, ways to encourage students to study physics, and students' enthusiasm for courses in foreign language and literature. AA, DI, EX, PA, RU, SU, U, W

188. Light, Richard J., Singer, Judith D., & Willett, John B. (1990). *By design: Planning research in higher education.* Cambridge, MA: Harvard University Press. 272 pp.

This handbook for studying higher education is written for people who have little or no technical training in evaluation research. The authors stress careful research design as a key to success. Using over fifty examples of actual studies, and the experience of the Harvard Assessment Seminars, the authors lead readers through a series of basic questions such as "What are your questions?," "What groups do you want to study?," and "What are your outcomes?" They introduce foundational concepts and principles for a productive study. BI, EV, EX, H, TH

189. Linn, Robert L. (1993). *Educational measurement.* Phoenix, AZ: Oryx. 610 pp.

Sponsored by the National Council for Measurement in Education and the American Council on Education, this third edition of a standard reference contains 18 chapters written by experts in the field of measurement. Each chapter reviews current technical knowledge and professional practice in one area of measurement and is applicable to all levels of schooling. Chapters are arranged in three parts: theory and general principles; construction, administration, and scoring; and applications. DV, E, EV, I, PC, PR, T, TC, U

190. Loacker, Georgine. (1991). *Designing a national assessment system: Alverno's institutional perspective.* Milwaukee, WI: Alverno College. 60 pp.

One of a series of papers commissioned by the U.S. Department of Education in support of a national assessment of college student learning, in connection with developing the National Education Goal of Literacy and Adult Learning, the paper summarizes what Alverno College faculty have learned about assessing and improving the quality of student learning. The author applies these principles to the development of a national assessment, arguing that a national assessment should contribute to improvement of learning in institutions and to accountability. This paper can be read in conjunction with Mentkowski, 1991, a second paper applying the Alverno experience to national assessment. A, AY, BI, CD, CE, CR, CT, EX, G, GE, H, I, IN, LS, MT, NT, O, OA, OS, PG, PR, RR, S, TH

191. Lockart, Daniel C. (Ed.). (1984). *Making effective use of mailed questionnaires.* New Directions for Program Evaluation, No. 21. San Francisco: Jossey-Bass. 102 pp.

This book describes how to use mailed questionnaires effectively in a variety of situations, including how to increase return rate. EV, MT, RR, S, TH

192. Love, Patrick G. (1995). Exploring the impact of student affairs professionals on student outcomes. *Journal of College Student Development, 36,* 162-170.

This article is a synthesis of research and literature about the influence of student affairs professionals on student outcomes. The author examines conceptual frameworks which include the importance of out-of-class experiences, importance of interaction with faculty, and research on student socialization. He also explores the evidence of direct influence of student affairs professionals and paraprofessionals on student outcomes. Inherent methodological challenges are presented for consideration. OA, PV, SN

193. Ludeman, Roger B., & Fisher, Richard. (1989). Breathe life into student life departments with CPR: Comprehensive Program Review. *NASPA Journal, 26,* 248-255.

The authors contend that effective higher education planning involves all divisions and departments. A proposed five-year cycle integrates planning and evaluation of a student affairs division with broader institutional efforts. This cycle includes annual reports, consumer evaluations, comprehensive program reviews, institutional strategic planning, needs analyses, and student opinion surveys. The comprehensive program review (CPR) is highlighted as the "pivotal process" in this planning review cycle. Comprehensive program review includes preparation, departmental self-study, evaluation, external review, strategic planning, and implementation. D, PE, PL, SL, SN, SP

194. MacGregor, Jean (Ed.). (1993). *Student self-evaluation: Fostering reflective learning.* New Directions for Teaching and Learning, No. 56. San Francisco: Jossey-Bass. 123 pp.

Six chapters by various authors explore aspects of student self-evaluation (SSE): an introduction and rationale, description of purposes and settings, student difficulties, supported conditions, relationship of SSE to outcome assessment, and effects of SSE on student development. An appendix provides prompts and assignments, examples of SSE essays, and resources. A, C, CO, CT, EX, FE, H, I, MT, OA, PR, SA, SU, TH, U, W

195. Mager, Robert F. (1984). *Goal analysis.* Belmont, CA: Pitman Learning. 139 pp.

This humorous book presents a step-by-step method for identifying important outcomes and framing technically effective statements of outcome goals. G, H, OS, SS, TH

196. Mager, Robert F. (1984). *Measuring instructional results: Or got a match?* Belmont, CA: David S. Lake. 166 pp.

This elementary introduction focuses on assessing the achievement of instructional objectives. C, H, OA

197. Mager, Robert F. (1984). *Preparing instructional objectives.* Belmont, CA: Lake. 136 pp.

The author's approach to developing instructional objectives has had a significant impact on education since the 1962 edition of this classic. His book is a step-by-step guide for formulating technically effective statements of the intended results of instruction. C, G, H, O, OS, SS, TA, TH

198. Marchese, Ted. (1985, September). Learning about assessment. *AAHE Bulletin, 38*(1), 10-13.

This article describes AAHE's first involvement in outcome assessment in the early days of the assessment movement. The author reviews the background pressures on colleges and universities for assessment, the meaning and various manifestations of assessment, and the institutions involved in assessment at the time. HP, OA

199. Marchese, Ted. (1985, November/December). Let's reward quality: Tennessee's bold experiment. *Change, 17*(6), 37-45.

Change's executive editor interviews several officials concerning the genesis and functioning of the State of Tennessee's performance funding policy for its public institutions of higher education. AY, OA, SW

200. Marcus, Laurence R., Leone, Anita O., & Goldberg, Edward D. (1983). *The path to excellence: Quality assurance in higher education* (ASHE-ERIC Higher Education Research Report No. 1). Washington, DC: Association for the Study of Higher Education. 68 pp.

This book reviews the history of government involvement in higher education, accreditation, the case for institutional self-regulation, and the role of assessment in self-regulation as a means for providing assurance of quality. AR, AY, HP, OA, PE, SS, SW

201. Marsh, H. W. (1984). Students' evaluations of university teaching: dimensionality, reliability, validity, potential biases, and utility. *Journal of Educational Psychology, 76*(5), 707-754.

The author reviews research designs and findings concerning students' evaluations of teaching. He establishes the reliability and multidimensionality of student evaluations of instruction, their freedom from effects of biasing variables, their reflection of characteristics of the instruction, and their usefulness for personnel decisions and professional development. BI, EI, FA, PA, U

202. Marshall, Max S. (1968). *Teaching without grades.* Corvallis: Oregon State University Press. 144 pp.

A medical school professor shares his ideas about grades and his experiences of teaching for 30 years without grades. GD, SI

203. McClain, Charles J. (1991, April/May). Education with integrity: The role of assessment. *AACJC Journal, 61*(5), 49-52.

The author argues for outcome assessment, especially in the community college. He enumerates important changes in the social environment, describes benefits that can accrue from an effective assessment program for improving learning, and stresses the need for leadership. CC, IW, OA, SC, VA

204. McClenney, Kay M. (1990, September/October). Whither assessment? Commitments needed for meaningful change. *Change, 22*(5), 54.

The author, an official at the Education Commission of the States, offers four principles for assessment to be effective in serving society's needs. AY, OA, SW

205. McLeod, P. J. (1987, August). Faculty assessments of case reports of medical students. *Journal of Medical Education, 62*(8), 673-677.

The author studied inter-rater reliability when scoring case reports written by medical students of 17 members of the McGill University Faculty of Medicine who had "extensive teaching and assessment experience" (p. 673) in reading student case reports. Number of comments made on a report ranged from zero to 40, and global ratings ranged from 60 to 95. Without specific guidelines for the global ratings, different readers rated some reports both excellent and very poor. Only two of 595 errors were agreed upon by more than 50 percent of the faculty raters. The author emphasizes the need for "clear, valid, and consistent feedback that does not confuse" (p. 677) and interfere with learning. As a result of the study, faculty explored the use of standard criteria and assessment formats and training in assessment. CL, CR, DI, EI, GD, MT, PA, SI, TC

206. McMillan, James H. (Ed.). (1988). *Assessing students' learning*. New Directions for Teaching and Learning, No. 34. San Francisco: Jossey-Bass. 108 pp.

An introductory chapter discusses basic issues and principles of classroom assessment. Other chapters describe using assessment to improve instruction, assessing critical thinking across the curriculum, writing, experiential learning, and the departmental major field of study. Final chapters treat the grading of students and provide an editor's synthesis and recommendations. C, CD, CT, EI, GR, M, OA, U, W

207. Mehrens, William A., & Lehmann, Irwin J. (1984). *Measurement and evaluation in education and psychology*. New York: Holt, Rinehard, and Winston. 658 pp.

This book, a basic textbook for measurement and evaluation in education, covers purposes of measurement and evaluation in education, technical aspects of evaluation, teacher-made evaluations, standardized methods of evaluation, and communication of results of evaluation. C, EV, I, IS, MT, PR, ST, TC, TH

208. Mentkowski, Marcia. (1991). Creating a context where institutional assessment yields educational improvement. *Journal of General Education, 40*, 255-283.

The author addresses faculty concerns about introducing outcome assessment into a department or institution and details six guidelines for developing a supportive institutional context in which assessment can produce optimally useful results. She describes assessment as "values in action." CR, OA, SC, U

209. Mentkowski, Marcia. (1991). *Designing a national assessment system: Assessing abilities that connect education and work*. Milwaukee, WI: Alverno College. 72 pp.

One of a series of papers prepared for the U.S. Department of Education, this report summarizes Alverno College's lessons from its research on the relationship of the College's student outcomes and the work experience of its graduates. The author describes principles for a national assessment of college outcomes, recommendations, implications, issues, and questions. The author discusses what and how to assess abilities in the context of developing means of assessing higher-order thinking and communication skills for the National Education Goal of Literacy and Adult Learning. This paper can be read in conjunction with Loacker, 1991, a second paper applying the Alverno experience to national assessment. A, AY, BI, CD, CE, CR, CT, EX, G, GE, H, I, IN, LS, MT, NT, O, OA, OS, PG, PR, RR, S, TH

210, Mentkowski, Marcia, & Doherty, Austin. (1984). *Careering after college: Establishing the validity of abilities learned in college for later careering and professional performance*. Milwaukee, WI: Alverno College Productions. 222 pp.

This is the second edition of the "overarching" report in the Careering After College series which reports on assessment practices in the outcome-based curriculum at Alverno College. In this volume the authors provide an overview of the series and summary of research results. Topics include the importance of focusing on and validating outcomes in higher education; defining, assessing, and validating student development outcomes; indicators (measures) of cognitive development, learning style, and performance; defining and assessing outcomes at Alverno College; establishing the validity of outcomes; research objectives and methods; the actual outcomes of the Alverno College experience, including student change; relating the Alverno outcomes to the world of work; and important learning from the research. Other sections include new directions for research, abstracts of Alverno research reports, and extensive references. A, BI, CD, CO, CR, CT, CU, EX, FR, G, GE, IN, IS, LS, MT, O, OA, PG, RR, SC, SU, TH, U

211. Mentkowski, Marcia, Rogers, Glen, Deemer, Deborah, Ben-Ur, Tamar, Reisetter, Judy, Rickards, William, & Talbott, Mary. (1991, April 5). *Understanding abilities, learning and development through college outcomes studies: What can we expect from higher education assessment?* Paper presented at the American Educational Research Association, Chicago. 178 pp.

This is a summary of research methodology and findings on student development at Alverno College and a compilation of data and materials developed at the College. Together, these discussions and materials present an overview of possibilities using assessment to inform practice in colleges and universities. A, AO, BI, CD, CO, CR, CT, CU, EX, GE, I, IA, IN, IR, IS, LS, MS, MT, O, OA, OS, RR, SC, U

212. Mentkowski, Marcia, & Strait, Michael J. (1983). *A longitudinal study of student change in cognitive development, learning styles, and generic abilities in an outcome-centered liberal arts curriculum.* Milwaukee, WI: Alverno College Productions. 357 pp.

This report is a detailed description of cross-sectional and longitudinal studies of student development at Alverno College. The overarching study addressed three questions about changes in students in the competencies reflecting cognitive development, learning style, and other generic abilities, changes that can be attributed to the curriculum, and lessons that can assist institutions in improving their curricula. Included is detailed information on the unique Alverno learning process; research objectives; indicators (measures) used for, among other variables, intellectual development, ego development, moral reasoning, critical thinking, and learning style; sampling and data collection procedures; data analysis plan and methods; results; discussion; and summary. Appendices include the correspondence to constituents and other impedimenta of the research. A, BI, CD, CO, CT, CU, EX, GE, IN, IS, LS, MT, OA, PG, RR, SC, SU, TH, U

213. Miller, Richard I. (1979). *The assessment of college performance.* San Francisco: Jossey-Bass. 374 pp.

The author provides a comprehensive review of the process of institutional self-study. Included are planning an effective self-study; assessing the relevance of institutional objectives, the degree of student learning, faculty effective-

ness, existing and planned programs, adequacy of support staff and facilities, administrative leadership, fiscal management, governing-board operation, and external relations; developing a commitment to self-improvement; and instituting comprehensive evaluation. Also included are appendices reviewing comparative studies of graduate and professional schools and institution-wide studies, and an annotated bibliography. AD, AY, BI, EX, FA, G, GD, H, HP, IR, IW, O, PE, SC, SL, TH, TT

214. Milton, Ohmer. (1982). *Will that be on the final?* Springfield, IL: Charles C Thomas. 87 pp.

This review of research on classroom tests in American higher education raises serious concerns about outcome assessment. Problems of validity and reliability in many teacher-made, classroom tests call into question judgments based on their results. Both tests made by teachers and supplied by textbook publishers tend to assess memory and low-level comprehension at the expense of application and higher-order cognitive skills. Test items that require higher-order thinking are relatively rare. C, CD, MT, OA, PR, TC, TH

215. Milton, Ohmer. (1992). We must think anew. *Journal on Excellence in College Teaching, 3,* 19-32.

This article is a critical examination of several key assumptions about learning and teaching held by faculty, administrators, students, and the public. Focusing on classroom tests, symbol (grading) systems, and GPAs, the author concludes that these three factors distort the learning-teaching enterprise in higher education. C, GR, I, OA, PR, TC, TN

216. Milton, Ohmer, & Edgerly, John W. (1976). *The testing and grading of students.* New Rochelle, NY: Change Magazine. 62 pp.

This *Change* policy paper reviews the status of classroom tests and grading practices in American higher education. Both the American Association of University Professors and the Association of American Colleges endorsed the monograph "for its serviceability." Topics discussed include problems with testing, setting learning goals, test construction, grading, ways of addressing concerns about testing, and further reading. An annotated bibliography is included. BI, C, GR, MT, OA, PR, TH

217. Milton, Ohmer, Pollio, Howard R., & Eison, James A. (1986). *Making sense of college grades.* San Francisco: Jossey-Bass. 287 pp.

In this comprehensive examination of the grading system, the authors review the history of grades in the United States; describe national survey of attitudes towards grades (with a total of 6,165 respondents); review other available research, including research with the LOGO II instrument on the differences in behavior between learning-oriented and grade-oriented students; and give suggestions about grading practices. Two appendices present the national survey instrument and its resultant data. The reference list dealing with grades is extensive. A, BI, GR, HP, I, IN, IS, LN, MT, RR

218. Morante, Edward A. (1990). Assessing collegiate outcomes. In Laurence R. Marcus & Benjamin D. Stickney (Eds.), *Politics and policy in the age of education* (pp. 125-148). Springfield, IL: Charles C Thomas.

The director of the New Jersey Statewide College Outcomes Evaluation Program provides an overview of state assessment efforts. He reviews the need for assessment and external forces affecting higher education's need to focus on accountability. The author describes the scope of outcome assessment and distinguishes it from assessment of basic skills. He discusses the leadership role played by state government, performance indicators defined across the state and by individual institutions, key indicators, ways to implement a state assessment program, and models of state assessment from Florida, Tennessee, Virginia, and New Jersey. A, AY, GE, IE, M, MT, OA, PI, SW, TH

219. Morante, Edward A. (1991). *General Intellectual Skills (GIS) assessment in New Jersey*. Washington, DC: National Center for Education Statistics. (ERIC Document Reproduction Service No. ED 340 760)

This paper was commissioned by the U.S. Department of Education as background for a study design workshop for a national assessment of college student learning held in November 1991. It describes the New Jersey College Basic Skills Placement Test used to assess the basic skills of entering students, and the College Outcomes Evaluation Program (COEP), a comprehensive plan for assessing students' learning in general education and major fields and their personal development, faculty members' scholarship and creative expression, and institutions' community and social impact. The program included the New Jersey General Intellectual Skills Assessment (now the ETS Tasks in Critical Thinking), an assessment of critical thinking, problem solving, quantitative reasoning, and writing. Included are the comments of three reviewers. (ERIC) A, BS, CD, CS, CT, GE, IS, M, NT, OA, SW, W

220. Moxley, Linda S. (1988). The role and impact of a student affairs research and evaluation office. *NASPA Journal, 25,* 174-179.

This article describes the purpose and value of a research and evaluation office within a division of student affairs. The author discusses in detail the goals and objectives of the strategic plan for such an office at the University of Texas at Arlington. The impact of the information col-

lected through this office is described using specific examples of previously completed research and evaluation projects. The projects cover the breadth of student affairs, including retention, residence halls, student organizations, budget analyses, computer issues, staff issues, and student fees. AO, D, SN, SP, U

221. Muffo, John A. (1992). The status of student outcomes assessment at NASULGC member institutions. *Research in Higher Education, 33*(6), 765-774.

This paper reports the results of a Spring 1990 survey of NASULGC member institutions concerning their use of and experience with outcome assessment. Of 73 institutions that responded, only 6 (8.2 percent) had neither any assessment in place nor were planning for assessment. Most plans were "embryonic," however. Thirty percent reported some changes on campus due to assessment. "[I]t appeared that the most prestigious universities were the least likely to respond and, when they did respond, were the least likely to be positive regarding outcomes assessment efforts" (p. 773). AY, PR, RU, SC, SW

222. Muffo, John A., & McLaughlin, Gerald W. (Eds.). (1987). *A primer on institutional research.* Tallahassee, FL: Association for Institutional Research. 133 pp.

The 15 authorities who contribute to this handbook, produced by the Association for Institutional Research, introduce readers to 10 fundamental areas in the field of institutional research. Chapters review principles of longitudinal enrollment analysis—retention, attrition, and student flow studies; needs assessment; program evaluation; budgeting and financial planning; economic impact; support for self-studies; institutional comparisons; the institutional fact book; and use of statistical packages and spreadsheets. (Also see Whiteley, 1992.) HB, IC, IR, NA, PE, ST, SY

223. Musil, Caryn McTighe (Ed.). (1992). *Students at the center: Feminist assessment.* Washington, DC: Association of American Colleges and National Women's Studies Association. 120 pp.

This book explores the impact of women's studies programs on students and the application of outcome assessment to these programs, based on a project conducted by the two publishing organizations. Chapters include an introduction and description of project history, the assessment movement, and feminism; feminist theory and assessment; feminist assessment; the design of assessment; a review of methods and models of assessment; brief accounts from various institutions; and three appendices with sample student, alumnae, and faculty questionnaires, a directory of feminist consultants, and a selected bibliography. BI, DI, EX, IS, MT, OA, SC

224. Nettles, Michael T. (Ed.). (1990). *The effect of assessment on minority student participation.* New Directions for Institutional Research, No. 65. San Francisco: Jossey-Bass. 110 pp.

Seven chapters by various authors discuss assessment and minority group students. Included are standardized test performance, assessment politics, diversity within Asian and Pacific American student populations, implications of diversity for institutional research, assessing program effectiveness in institutions with diverse student populations, the effects of assessment on minority participation and achievement, and minority student attitudes toward mathematics as a variable that can compound their disadvantage. CE, DV, EX, IR, PE, PR, SC

225. Nichols, James O. (1995a). *A practitioner's handbook for institutional effectiveness and student outcomes assessment implementation.* New York: Agathon Press. 280 pp.

This handbook is a cookbook for persons on a college or university campus responsible for implementation of institutional effectiveness or outcomes assessment. Description of an Institutional Effectiveness Implementation Model is followed by discussions of institutional activities during the first year of assessment: developing a statement of institutional purpose, conducting attitudinal surveys, choosing cognitive assessment instruments, assessing behavioral change and performance, and using existing data from institutional data systems. A chapter about department level assessment includes sections on using statements of outcomes (objectives) in academic and nonacademic units, assessing general education, and relating assessment and Continuous Quality Improvement. Chapters focus on beginning assessment in the two-year college, an annual effectiveness cycle, and long-term maintenance of effectiveness operations. Five appendices have a process for designing and examples of statements of purpose, and a description of a program review process. CC, CD, CE, CQ, D, DB, G, GE, GN, H, I, IN, IR, IS, IW, LI, M, MS, MT, O, OA, OS, PE, SL, TH, U

226. Nichols, James O. (1995b). *Assessment case studies: Common issues in implementation with various campus approaches to resolution.* New York: Agathon Press. 212 pp.

Using the experience with assessment on 11 diverse campuses representing most institutional types, this book describes important assessment issues and methods.

Chapters introduce a generic model of institutional effectiveness and assessment, describe how to lay a foundation for institutional effectiveness or assessment of outcomes, provide a detailed design at the level of department or program, describe how to establish an institutional effectiveness or assessment cycle on campus, and provide conclusions and summary findings from the case study institutions. Nine appendices contain examples of intended educational outcomes, means of assessment, and criteria for success from many disciplines; examples of mission statements; and other campus documents and plans. CC, CD, D, DI, EX, GN, H, HP, IW, LA, M, MS, MT, O, OA, OS, RU, TH, U

227. Nichols, James O. (1995c). *The departmental guide and record book for student outcomes assessment and institutional effectiveness.* New York: Agathon Press. 80 pp.

This handbook helps academic, administrative, or educational support departments develop statements of intended student outcomes, assess student learning, and use the results of assessment to improve instruction. The author provides the background about the role of assessment at the department level and contends that if assessment is to work, it must work in an institution's departments. Two appendices describe assessment record book forms and their use. D, G, H, MT, O, P, U

228. Northeast Missouri State University. (1984). *In pursuit of degrees with integrity: A value added approach to undergraduate assessment.* Washington, DC: American Association of State Colleges and Universities. 95 pp.

The program of value-added assessment at Northeast Missouri State University (now Truman State University) is described in this book. Among others, chapters include the case for the value-added concept—knowing the change an institution or program makes, or value it adds, to student development—planning for value added; and the future of value added. EX, MO, MT, OA, SR, TH, VA

229. Nummedal, Susan G. (1991). *Designing a process to assess higher order thinking and communication skills in college graduates: Issues of concern.* Washington, DC: National Center for Education Statistics. (ERIC Document Reproduction Service No. ED 340 761)

This paper was commissioned by the U.S. Department of Education as background for a study design workshop for a national assessment of college student learning held in November 1991. The author suggests that any national assessment of critical thinking skills may find relatively little help from current assessments, that a national assessment should focus on practical skills and dispositions, that a wide range of experts should be involved in developing such an assessment, and that assessment should be focused on improving learning and teaching. Included are the comments of three reviewers. (ERIC) BI, CD, CT, NT, OA, PR

230. O'Banion, Terry. (1994). Guidelines for auditing the effectiveness of teaching and learning. In Terry O'Banion & Associates (Eds.), *Teaching & learning in the community college* (pp. 301-317). Washington, DC: American Association of Community Colleges.

The author reviews research showing a radical gap between the value faculty place on teaching and their perceptions of the degree to which their institutions reward it. The author provides a detailed framework for auditing an institution's policies that tend to increase or decrease the effectiveness of its teaching. AU, AY, CA, CC, EI, IW, PE

231. Pace, C. Robert. (1979). *Measuring outcomes of college: Fifty years of findings and recommendations for the future.* San Francisco: Jossey-Bass. 188 pp.

This book reviews accumulated research on higher education, specifically of student achievement during and after college, and of institutions as organizations and environments in which to live and study, up to the beginning of the modern assessment movement. The author provides an historical review of major studies and programs to assess higher education institutions. In an epilogue, he makes suggestions for future assessment research needs. FR, HP, IW, OA, PG

232. Pascarella, Ernest T. (Ed.). (1982). *Studying student attrition.* New Directions for Institutional Research, No. 36. San Francisco: Jossey-Bass. 104 pp.

Seven chapters by various authors describe methods for studying student attrition (withdrawal from college) and using the results. Included are a definition of *dropout*, conceptual models of attrition, selecting the variables to measure and measurement concerns, designing studies, designing interventions to reduce attrition and verifying their effectiveness, and additional resources for research on attrition. BI, HB, IR, LS, MT, TH

233. Pascarella, Ernest T., & Terenzini, Patrick T. (1991). *How college affects students: Findings and insights from twenty years of research.* San Francisco: Jossey-Bass. 894 pp.

This book is a comprehensive resource for understanding student development in college and its assessment. The authors provide a review of 2,600 studies of college effects on students concluded during the last two decades. Summarizing the results of these studies, the authors critique the diverse methodologies and give their own best judgment about the meaning of the findings. Introductory chapters provide an overview and describe the organization of the research in the book and a review of theories and models of student change in college. Student outcomes reviewed include verbal, quantitative, and subject matter competence; cognitive skills and intellectual growth; changes in identity, self-concept, and self-esteem; relating to others and the external world; attitudes and values; moral development, educational attainment, and

career choice and development; economic benefits; and quality of life after college. In two final chapters the authors summarize research and give the implications of the findings for policy and practice. An appendix discusses technical methodological issues of assessment and analysis. A, BI, CD, CR, CT, DV, E, EV, FR, GE, HP, I, IC, IE, IN, MT, OA, PR, ST, SU, TC, TH, VA

234. Paskow, J. (Ed.). (1988). *Assessment programs and projects: A directory.* Washington, DC: American Association for Higher Education Assessment Forum. 82 pp.

This directory of diverse institutions and other organizations that were engaged in assessment activities at the time of publication includes sections written by members of these institutions and organizations. Each section includes information about the institution, the purposes of assessment in the organization, background information, key features of the program, assessment strategies and instruments, impact of assessment, next steps planned, costs, resources, and the names of people to contact for further information. AS, CC, CO, EX, IS, LA, MT, OA, SC, SI, RU, U

235. Patrick, John, & Niles, Spencer G. (1988). Establishing accountability and evaluation procedures in student affairs offices. *NASPA Journal, 25,* 291-296.

As the pressures and demands for accountability grow, evaluation holds greater importance for student affairs professionals. The authors discuss several roadblocks to be minimized in the establishment of accountability and evaluation procedures. They also stress the importance of staff participation and commitment for evaluation results to be included in future decision-making processes. Three steps toward effective evaluation are suggested: identifying program goals and objectives, collecting data, and compiling a final report. G, PR, SN

236. Patton, Gerald W., Dasher-Alston, Robin, Ratteray, Oswald M. T., & Kait, Mary Beth. (1996). *Outcomes assessment in the middle states region: A report on the 1995 outcomes assessment survey.* Philadelphia, PA: Middle States Association of Colleges and Schools, Commission on Higher Education. 23 pp.

This report describes the results of a Middle States Association survey conducted in 1995 of 495 member colleges and universities to ascertain progress with outcomes assessment. The rate of response was 68 percent. Fifty-seven percent of respondents do not yet "have an institution-wide plan;" 34 percent have had a plan for three years

or longer. Institutions with plans claimed to utilize direct measures of "institutional effectiveness, but few emphasize direct measures of teaching and learning. . . . Faculty resistance and a lack of sufficient human and financial resources are the chief barriers to implementing new assessment activities or sustaining existing initiatives."
AC, AY, IW, MT, OA

237. Paul, Richard, & Nosich, Gerald. (1991). *A proposal for the national assessment of higher-order thinking at the community college, college, and university levels.* Washington, DC: National Center for Education Statistics. (ERIC Document Reproduction Service No. 340 762)

This paper was commissioned by the U.S. Department of Education as background for a study design workshop for a national assessment of college student learning held in November 1991. The authors formulate 21 criteria that should be met by a national assessment of critical thinking, describe their concept of critical thinking, and provide a framework and timetable for assessment, and two appendices with additional materials. Included are critiques of the report by three reviewers. (ERIC) BI, CD, CT, NT, OA

238. Peacock, Dennis E. (1994, June 1) . *Beyond academic outcomes: Expanding into comprehensive assessment while preserving faculty ownership.* Paper presented at the 34th Annual Forum, Association for Institutional Research, New Orleans, LA. 12 pp. (ERIC Document Reproduction Service No. ED 373 630)

The director of assessment and testing at Northeast Missouri State University (now Truman State University) describes efforts to expand outcome assessment beyond cognitive development to important non-cognitive outcomes. The author suggests guidelines for aiding faculty acceptance of this broadened scope of assessment. A, EX, IW, OA, SC, SN

239. Peters, Roger. (1994, November/December). Some snarks are boojums: Accountability and the end(s) of higher education. *Change, 26*(6), 16-23.

The author reviews problems of institutions in responding effectively to state accountability mandates and enumerates potential damaging effects of accountability on education. "Effective assessment requires a diligent search for bad news, which is more useful than good, but accountability encourages the opposite" (p. 18). The author suggests ways by which institutions can improve the situation.
AY, IW, OA

240. Peterson, Marvin W., Cameron, Kim S., Knapp, Andrea, Spencer, Melinda G., & White, Theodore H. (1991). *Assessing the organizational and administrative context for teaching and learning: An institutional self-study manual.* Ann Arbor, MI: University of Michigan, National Center for Research to Improve Postsecondary Teaching and Learning. 102 pp.

This manual provides a conceptual overview of the organizational context for teaching and learning, provides a guide for developing a case study guide of the management context on a campus, and describes how to use the Academic Management Practices Inventory to understand and improve the organizational context. AD, CM, H, IN, IR, IS, IW, MG, MT, PA, SC, TH

241. Phillips, S. E. (1993). Legal issues in performance assessment. *Education Law Quarterly, 2*(2), 329-358.

The author, an attorney, reviews legal issues involved in high-stakes assessment and evaluation. Citing case law throughout, his specific, detailed discussion relevant to all levels of schooling includes historical perspectives; various types of assessments dealing with students and faculty; technical, psychometric issues; potential future legal challenges; and advice to designers of assessments. CE, ET, EV, HP, I, IA, L, OA, PA, PC, PR, S, SE, TC

242. Pike, Gary R. (1992). The components of construct validity: A comparison of two measures of general education outcomes. *Journal of General Education, 41,* 130-159.

Based on the COMP Objective Test and College BASE as used at the University of Tennessee-Knoxville, this article provides specific criteria for faculty members when evaluating the utility of both commercially available and locally constructed assessments of students' outcomes. In addition to statistical analyses (validity and reliability) of the tests' results, the author provides both faculty and student opinion on coverage of content, critical thinking skills, and attitudes and values by both tests. GE, I, IS, MT, RU, TC

243. Pike, Gary R. (1995). The relationship between self reports of college experiences and achievement test scores. *Research in Higher Education, 36*(1), 1-21.

A study of the usefulness of student self-reports as proxy indicators of academic learning and college experiences for a national assessment of college student outcomes suggests they "should be used with care as proxies for a national test" but may be useful "as policy indicators to improve undergraduate education" (p. 1). MT, NT, TH

244. Pollio, Howard R., & Humphries, W. Lee. (1988). Grading students. In James J. McMillan (Ed.), *Assessing students' learning.* New Directions for Teaching and Learning, No. 34 (pp. 85-97). San Francisco: Jossey-Bass.

This brief resume of the territory covered by Milton, Pollio, and Eison (1986) includes recommendations. GR

245. Prager, Carolyn (Ed.). (1993). *Accreditation of the two-year college.* New Directions for Community Colleges, No. 83. San Francisco: Jossey-Bass. 107 pp.

Ten chapters by various authors discuss regional accreditation of two-year colleges, accreditation of branch campuses, general education in career curricula, cost-benefit analyses of accreditation, accreditation and outcome assessment in the open-ended institution, the leadership role of the president in building consensus for accreditation, the impact of accreditation on small colleges, institutionalizing outcome assessment, and challenges and opportunities in accreditation. A final chapter provides an annotated bibliography of works on accreditation. AR, AY, CC, HP, IW, MT, OA

246. Ratcliff, James L. (1991). *What type of national assessment fits American higher education.* University Park, PA: Pennsylvania State University.

This paper was commissioned by the U.S. Department of Education as background for a study design workshop for a national assessment of college student learning held in November 1991. The author discusses various needs for development of an effective national assessment of college students' learning, including building on the experience of state assessment programs, involving faculty widely during development, and use by institutions and their faculty. A variety of methods is suggested for both short- and long-term use. Included are the comments of four reviewers. (ERIC) BI, CD, CT, NT, OA, PA, PR, SW, TR

247. Ratcliff, James L. (1995). Putting students at the center of statewide assessment plans. In Thomas A. Angelo & Monica M. Manning (Eds.), *Improving learning: Forging better connections between assessment, quality, & accreditation. Commissioned papers for the 10th annual Conference on Assessment & Quality.* Washington, DC: American Association for Higher Education.

The author gives a rationale for statewide assessment, reviews research on institutional variation in student learning, and urges states to put student learning at the center of their assessment plans. AY, IW, OA, S, SW

248. Ratcliff, James L., Jones, Elizabeth A., & Hoffman, Steven. (1992). *Handbook on linking assessment and general education.* University Park, PA: Pennsylvania State University, National Center on Postsecondary Teaching, Learning, & Assessment. 116 pp.

This handbook describes a Coursework Cluster Analysis Model (CCAM) for linking the curriculum with student learning. The method employs statistical analysis of student transcripts to discover patterns of course work related to specific student outcomes. Analysis identifies courses with powerful effects on student learning for particular groups of students with particular input characteristics, courses not making powerful contributions which can be

modified or eliminated, and results that contribute important information for academic advising. The authors review the literature on transcript analysis and describe the statistical methods used in the Model. Two appendices describe catalog studies—determining an institution's student requirements and describing patterns of changes in courses, such as additions and deletions for the sample of students, and provide the specific SPSS commands for the CCAM processes. CD, CU, DB, DV, GE, H, IN, IS, MT, OA, PA, ST, T, TH, U, VA

249. Rau, William, & Leonard, Wilbert M., II. (1990). Evaluating Ph. D. sociology programs: Theoretical, methodological and policy implications. *American Sociologist, 21*(3), 232-256.

The authors report a study of 60 doctoral programs in sociology on six measures of research productivity and graduate education. They show deficiencies in traditional rankings and add dimensions to these evaluations. They suggest a "conflict between faculty productivity and graduate education" and "that omission of several assessment variables may have penalized departments emphasizing qualitative research" (p. 232). They provide recommendations for improved evaluation. AY, CR, D, FR, GD, HP, IA, IC, NT, OA, PE, RU

250. Resnick, Daniel P., & Peterson, Natalie L. (1991). *Evaluating progress toward goal five: A report to the National Center for Education Statistics.* Washington, DC: National Center for Education Statistics. (ERIC Document Reproduction Service No. ED 340 764)

This paper was commissioned by the U.S. Department of Education as background for a study design workshop for a national assessment of college student learning held in November 1991. The authors state that multiple indicators are necessary for assessment of college students' higher-order skills and suggest specific indicators for six different areas. Included are comments by three reviewers. (ERIC) CD, IN, NT, OA

251. Rock, Donald A. (1991). *Development of a process to assess higher order thinking for college graduates.* Washington, DC: National Center for Education Statistics (ERIC Document Reproduction Service No. ED 340 765)

This paper was commissioned by the U.S. Department of Education as background for a study design workshop for a national assessment of college student learning held in November 1991. It discusses ways to measure and teach higher-order cognitive skills, scoring protocols that yield useful diagnostic information for instruction, development of free-response items, and setting of standards of performance. Included are the comments of three reviewers. (ERIC) CD, CT, EV, NT, OA, PR

252. Rodriguez, Raul G. (1992). Student tracking with a personal computer: An ongoing process. *AACJC Journal, 62*(4), 25-27.

This article describes issues raised and problems encountered during development of a PC-based student tracking system. BS, CC, DB, MT, PC, TC, TH, W

253. Roe, Ernest, & McDonald, Rod. (1984). *Informal professional judgment: A guide to evaluation in post-secondary education.* St. Lucia, Queensland, Australia: University of Queensland Press. 300 pp.

This detailed, comprehensive handbook focuses on the evaluation of courses, their units, and the quality of instruction. C, EI, FA, H, IT, IS, MT, PA, SC, TH

254. Roe, Ernest, McDonald, Rod, & Moses, Ingrid. (1986). *Reviewing academic performance: Approaches to the evaluation of departments and individuals.* Manchester, NH: University of Queensland Press. 341 pp.

This handbook examines assessing and evaluating academic departments and individual faculty members for purposes of professional development, personnel decisions, accreditation, consumer information for course selection by students, and communication with other stakeholders. Specific topics are background issues, procedures and policies, and collection of information for the review. Case studies and exercises are provided for both purposes. Two appendices contain academic review and graduate program review procedures. D, EI, EX, FA, GD, H, IT, MT, PE

255. Rogers, Gloria M., & Sando, Jean K. (1996). *Stepping ahead: An assessment plan development guide.* Terre Haute, IN: Rose-Hulman Institute of Technology. 15 pp.

This campus guide to assessment at Rose-Hulman introduces several basic concepts in assessment and evaluation and delineates and elaborates on a series of key steps in an assessment plan. The booklet includes two worksheets and an exercise for developing goals, objectives, performance criteria, and means of collecting data. Available from the

first author at Rose-Hulman Institute of Technology, 5500 Wabash Avenue, Terre Haute, IN 47803. CR, EX, G, GN, H, MT, O, OA

256. Rossmann, Jack E., & El-Khawas, Elaine. (1987). *Thinking about assessment: Perspectives for presidents and chief academic officers.* Washington, DC: American Council on Education and the American Association for Higher Education. 22 pp.

This monograph defines assessment and describes the reasons for and benefits of assessment. It provides general suggestions for developing effective assessment programs: establishing the role of leadership, organizing the effort, collecting data, estimating costs, developing a schedule, and using the results of assessment for maximum impact. AY, CA, SC, SW, U

257. Sacks, Peter. (1997, March/April). Standardized testing: Meritocracy's crooked yardstick. *Change, 29*(2), 24-31.

The author describes the role standardized tests of mental ability play in schools, colleges, and society, the anti-testing movement, the history of the development and use of standardized tests, the evidence for their ability to predict academic and life success, their correlation with socioeconomic class, their impact on learning, the business of test construction and sales, the costs of tests, and the implications of standardized testing for society. CA, HP, IS, S, U

258. Scott, Robert A. (Ed.). (1984). *Determining the effectiveness of campus services.* New Directions for Institutional Research, No. 41. San Francisco: Jossey-Bass. 93 pp.

Seven chapters by various authors discuss the importance of institutional self-study; ways to evaluate student services, a public relations office, and academic libraries; and ways to plan and assess relationships with industry. One chapter stresses negative feedback on performance as "a necessary precondition for organizational improvement." The editor provides a final chapter that contains suggestions for further reading. D, MD, MT, PA, PE, SL, TH

259. Scriven, Michael. (1991). *Multiple-rating items.* (ERIC Document Reproduction Service No. ED 340 768)

The author describes a type of test item format that, unlike multiple-choice items, requires a test-taker to rate every member of an array, rather than choosing one member from the array. He claims these multiple-rating items possess the simplicity and reliability of scoring and the capacity for wide coverage of multiple-choice items but avoid their weaknesses. The author suggests that most test items that assess cognitive levels higher than recall and that require choice should be transformed to a multiple-rating format. (ERIC) CD, EV, I, OA

260. Seldin, Peter. (1984). *Changing practices in faculty evaluation.* San Francisco: Jossey-Bass. 200 pp.

The author suggests that faculty evaluation programs at many colleges and universities are "seriously flawed." Chapters discuss fiscal crises and implications for the faculty; legal challenges to decisions on retention, tenure, and promotion; the results of a national study of current faculty evaluation; and comments on the causes and implications of changing approaches to evaluation. The conclusion describes how to design and implement a successful program of evaluation. An appendix presents the instrument used in the survey. EI, FA, IS, MT, PR, TH

261. Seldin, Peter. (1988). *Evaluating and developing administrative performance: A practical guide for academic leaders.* San Francisco: Jossey-Bass. 242 pp.

The author reviews changing expectations and roles for academic administrators; provides a rationale for evaluating administrators' professional performance; and describes ways to plan, implement, and manage a successful performance evaluation program. He discusses legal issues in evaluation, methods for developing administrators, and ways to evaluate and develop the president. Included are survey instruments for collecting data. An appendix contains benchmarks or principles for each chapter for evaluating and developing administrators. AD, BI, H, IS, MT, TH

262. Seldin, Peter. (1997). *The teaching portfolio: A practical guide to improved performance and promotion/tenure decisions.* Bolton, MA: Anker. 268 pp.

This second edition reflects the "explosive growth" of the teaching portfolio in American colleges and universities since 1991. The first chapter introduces the teaching portfolio and traces its spread through higher education. Five additional chapters describe the types and presentation of materials that can be included in portfolios; explain the mentor's role; lay out a seven-step process for constructing a portfolio; describe use of portfolios to improve teaching, for retention, tenure, and promotion, in grantsmanship, and by graduate students hunting for positions; answer frequently asked questions about portfolios; suggest ways of self-mentoring in the absence of a mentor; give estimates of time to prepare a portfolio; present lessons learned about portfolios; and include a bibliography. In six chapters faculty members from various disciplines and types of institutions describe experiences with portfolios, including 23 examples of portfolios. CA, CC, CO, EI, EX, FA, H, IN, MT, PA, PR, PT, RU, SC, SF, SI, SR, T, TH, U

263. Seldin, Peter, & Associates. (1993). *Successful use of teaching portfolios.* Bolton, MA: Anker. 212 pp.

Eight chapters by various authors introduce the teaching portfolio concept and describe the preparation of portfolios, the role of the mentor, portfolio use in nine institu-

tions, and evaluation of portfolios for personnel decisions. The book includes answers to common questions about portfolios, a roundtable discussion on the results of portfolios, and sample portfolios from various disciplines and institutions. EI, EX, H, MT, PT, SC, TH, U

264. Sims, Serbrenia J. (1992). *Student outcomes assessment: A historical review and guide to program development.* Westport, CT: Greenwood. 158 pp.

This book provides a brief overview of assessment in the United States. The first part contains definitions; the context for assessment; common practices; an historical review of outcomes assessment since 1918, including a review of Federal and state efforts concerning assessment of student outcomes; and a review of accrediting agencies and assessment. The second part provides guidelines for designing and implementing outcome assessment programs and evaluating the effectiveness of assessment initiatives. An appendix contains the U.S. Secretary of Education's criteria for accreditation and case studies from the State of Virginia, the College of William and Mary, and the American Assembly of Collegiate Schools of Business. AR, AY, BI, HP, MT, OA

265. Smith, Vardaman R., Ahmed, Ehsan, Brunton, Bruce, Kohen, Andrew I., Milliman, Scott, Rosser, Marina, & Stevens, Debra. (1992). Reviewing an economics curriculum in the context of university-wide reforms. *Journal of General Education, 41,* 160-176.

This article is a description of an academic department's attempt to "fashion a set of departmental objectives, operational definitions, and strategies for improvements" (p. 171) for its undergraduate program at James Madison University. CU, D, DI, EX, G, M, O, SC

266. Sorochty, Roger W. (1991). Planning and assessment equal accountability. *NASPA Journal, 28,* 355-361.

The author begins with a general discussion of human development theory as a basis for planning and assessment. The Student Developmental Task and Lifestyle Inventory (SDTLI) is presented as a planning tool to identify the developmental tasks of students. Information from the SDTLI forms the backbone of the planning, assessment, and accountability approach, during which student affairs staff members create programs, activities, and services that intentionally address aspects of students' growth. The conclusion explains ways the SDTLI can be used over time to assess the impact of the college experience. This planning and assessment program can provide feedback to students and can articulate the mission of a student affairs program to internal and external stakeholders. D, IS, PE, SN, SU

267. Stage, Frances K. & Associates. (1992). *Diverse methods for research and assessment of college students.* Alexandria, VA: American College Personnel Association. 140 pp.

A general introduction to multiple qualitative methods, this book addresses new ways to study college students. A variety of approaches and techniques, including nonreactive measures, case study, document analysis, historical analysis, ethnographic interview, and focus groups, are discussed in individual chapters. Multiple methods, quantitative or qualitative, are advised to obtain a more complete picture of college students. Examples demonstrate how methods can be used in action-oriented research and pure research. FR, I, MT, SN

268. Stark, Joan S., & Mets, Lisa A. (Eds.). (1988). *Improving teaching and learning through research.* New Directions for Institutional Research, No. 57. San Francisco: Jossey-Bass. 92 pp.

This series of papers considers various aspects of research on students and faculty members. Included are the role of institutional researchers, the effect of the organizational environment on student learning, course and program planning, the relationship of faculty motivation to teaching effectiveness, student motivation and cognition related to instruction, and future research directions. CD, FR, IR, LN, SC, U

269. Stark, Joan S., Shaw, Kathleen M., & Lowther, Malcolm A. (1989). *Student goals for college and courses: A missing link in assessing and improving academic achievement* (ASHE-ERIC Higher Education Report 6). Washington, DC: George Washington University. 119 pp.

This review of research stresses the importance of studying students' own goals. Chapters discuss reasons to study goals, current trends in assessing student goals, goals and their neglected attributes, concepts related to goals, and course-level goals as a missing link in improving teaching and learning. An appendix lists broad goal items from major surveys (CIRP, ETS, Centra, and NCHEMS) and details of some common typologies of student goals. BI, C, G, IA, IW, MT, RR, SU, TA, U

270. Stark, Joan S., & Thomas, Alice (Eds.). (1994). *Assessment and program evaluation.* Needham Heights, MA: Simon and Schuster. 823 pp.

This member of the ASHE Reader Series contains 73 articles and book chapters arranged in seven different sections: the need for and scope of assessment and program evaluation, the primary audiences for these activities, planning, the technical aspects of conducting studies, communicating and using results, evaluating the process, and examples. This collection of original literature covers most major issues raised by assessment and includes some contrary voices. AR, BI, C, CA, CQ, CT, DV, E, EV, EX, G, HP, M, MT, OA, PL, PR, SC, ST, SW, TH, U, VA

271. Steele, Joe M., & Lutz, David A. (1995). *Report of ACT's research on postsecondary assessment needs.* Iowa City, IA: ACT. 23 pp.

This paper reports results of a survey concerning current assessment activities, issues, and needs for assessment sent to the higher education commissions of all 50 states, the six regional accrediting associations, 223 state colleges and universities, 177 public two-year colleges, and 33 higher education agencies and associations. Implications from the survey results and a focus group are described, responses summarized, and a final statement provided of "What Must Change." Specific items asked about degree of state coordinating board support for the use of standardized assessments, questions to which state boards want answers, methods used by institutions to assess outcomes, problems involved in assessment, areas that should be assessed, skills currently inadequately assessed, degree of implementation so far, utility of a national assessment resource center, and usefulness of state accountability requirements. AR, AS, AY, CC, MO, OA, PR, RR, SR, SW

272. Stock, Patricia L., & Robinson, Jay L. (1987, May). Taking on testing: Teachers as tester-researchers. *English Education, 19*(2), 93-121.

This paper discusses conflicts between the assessment of writing and the way writing is taught and practiced in the classroom. Authors describe conflicting assumptions behind large-scale assessment and describe a project in which University of Michigan English faculty worked with high school English teachers to improve the assessment of writing. Included are questions that inform assessment, teacher-testers as readers of writing samples, placement of assessment at the local level, teachers reading and evaluating together, determination of ways to study assessment data, and research as conversation. MT, PA, PR, TN, W

273. *Successful student outcomes assessment: Six institutional case studies including the role of student affairs.* (1994). Washington, DC: National Association of Student Personnel Administrators. 23 pp.

This report describes the assessment programs at six colleges and universities chosen to demonstrate the role of student outcome assessment in improving programs and services. The report includes practical information about assessment methods and instruments, ways to use outcome data and information, and examples of institutional change and improvement resulting from the assessment process. The report concludes with a discussion and recommendations for student affairs professionals. Appendices include a student outcomes assessment study questionnaire, an inventory of assessment instruments used by participating institutions, and a selected bibliography on student outcomes assessment. B, CH, EX, IS, IW, OA, SN, U

274. Suskie, Linda A. (1996). *Questionnaire survey research: What works* (2nd ed.). Tallahassee, FL: Association for Institutional Research. 206 pp.

This comprehensive exploration of survey design research is written as a guide for novices and a reference tool for experts. The author takes the reader through a step-by-step understanding of planning a survey, developing the instrument, conducting the study, processing and analyzing the results, and using the information. H, IS

275. Tait, Jo, & Knight, Peter. (1995). Assessment and continuous quality improvement: A North American case study. *Innovations in Education and Training International, 32*(4), 356-361.

This article is a succinct description of a five-stage assessment process of academic and student services areas at James Madison University. Each stage is described, the strengths and weaknesses of the process outlined, and assessment related to staff development. AQ, CQ, EX, G, IW, PE, SC, SR, U

276. Task Force on Assessing the National Goal Relating to Postsecondary Education. (1992). *Report to the National Education Goals Panel* (92-07). Washington, DC: National Education Goals Panel. 21 pp. (ERIC Document Reproduction Service No. ED 349 897)

This report states National Education Goal 5 (now 6) and Objective 5 on critical thinking, communication, and problem solving; describes the purpose of assessing goal achievement; discusses the need for national standards and assessments of goal achievement, for coordination, and for an inventory of current assessment activities; and considers whether assessment is a federal, national, or state responsibility and whether assessing progress on Goal 5 should involve a comprehensive assessment that examines the

major features of institutions' performance together or a differentiated system that examines single dimensions of postsecondary performance. AY, G, NT, O

277. Terenzini, Patrick T. (1989). Assessment with open eyes: Pitfalls in studying student outcomes. *Journal of Higher Education, 60,* 644-664.

This article focuses on identifying potential problems in the creation of institution-wide assessment programs. Three major areas are addressed: definitional issues, organizational and implementational issues, and methodological issues. Definitional issues include the purpose of the assessment, the level of assessment, and the project being assessed. Issues include mobilizing support for the assessment effort, coordinating many people in an institution-wide effort, and determining the costs involved. Design limitations, measurement difficulties, and statistical hazards must all be addressed when considering methodological issues. The author provides a three-dimensional taxonomy of approaches to assessment. CA, IW, MT, OA, PR, SC, ST, TA, TC, TH

278. Terenzini, Patrick T., & Pascarella, Ernest T. (1991). Twenty years of research on college students: Lessons for future research. *Research in Higher Education, 32*(1), 83-92.

From a review of over 3,000 studies on students and college effects on students conducted since 1967, the authors describe eight lessons from their research, or eight tasks for researchers, that they consider essential for the improvement of future assessment research on student outcomes. (Also see Pascarella and Terenzini, 1991.) EV, FR, HP, OA, ST, TH

279. Theall, Michael, & Franklin, Jennifer (Eds.). (1990). *Student ratings of instruction: Issues for improving practice.* New Directions for Teaching and Learning, No. 43. San Francisco: Jossey-Bass. 135 pp.

Nine chapters by various authors review research and current practice in the student evaluation of instruction. Specific topics include the artistic and scientific performance of teachers, students' ratings in the context of complex systems of evaluation, operation of a faculty evaluation system, the problems and limits of using evaluation systems, ethical issues, communication of students' ratings to decision makers, dimensions of ratings to be used in making personnel decisions, differences among ratings in different academic fields and their relevance to personnel decisions, and continuing resistance to students' ratings in the face of their demonstrated validity and reliability. EI, ET, FA, MT, PR, TH

280. Thurman, Quint, & Malaney, Gary D. (1989). Surveying students as a means of assessing and changing policies and practices of student affairs programs. *NASPA Journal, 27,* 101-107.

The authors stress the importance of including students' voices in research and assessment on college campuses. At the University of Massachusetts at Amherst, a telephone survey project (Project Pulse) collects data reflective of the entire student body. After detailed description of the program, several examples of research studies using Project Pulse are discussed. The impact of assessment is illustrated through a description of policy and program changes resulting from the on-going data collection. CH, MO, SN

281. Tierney, William G. (Ed.). (1990). *Assessing academic climates and cultures.* New Directions for Institutional Research, No. 68. San Francisco: Jossey-Bass. 101 pp.

Seven chapters by various authors discuss understanding academic climate and culture as essential to the effectiveness of colleges and universities; using ethnographic audits to evaluate management; using surveys; and assessing student culture, faculty culture, and faculty values. One chapter addresses the importance of new presidents understanding their campus cultures, and a final chapter provides additional resources for analyzing, interpreting, and using campus culture and climate. AD, BI, CG, CM, MT, SC, TH

282. Trochim, William M. K. (1989). An introduction to concept mapping for planning and evaluation. *Evaluation and Program Planning, 12*(1), 1-16.

The author describes concept mapping, which shows relationships among concepts and helps students learn both concepts and relationships. Here concept mapping is used as a framework in a six-step process for guiding evaluation and planning. Concept mapping clarifies and speeds group work, produces a graphic representation of concepts and their relationships, and often improves group cohesiveness and morale. The author describes computer programs useful in the process. EV, MT, PL, T, TH

283. Upcraft, M. Lee, & Schuh, John H. (1996). *Assessment in student affairs: A guide for practitioners.* San Francisco: Jossey-Bass. 374 pp.

This inclusive guide through assessment helps the reader decide why assessment is important, what should be assessed, how to assess, and how to use the results. Part One sets the context for assessment in student affairs, including key questions to ask and information on qualita-

tive and quantitative methods. Part Two explores aspects of assessment in student affairs, including assessing student needs, student satisfaction, campus environments, student cultures, and programs and services. Part Three highlights challenges in doing assessment, including using the results and maintaining high standards of ethics and integrity. While written for student affairs practitioners, the book contains relevant information for anyone doing assessment, particularly those new to assessment. The Appendix is an annotated review of instruments for assessing student services, programs, and facilities. CG, D, ET, GN, H, I, IS, MT, NA, OA, PE, PG, SL, SN, SU, U

284. Venezky, Richard L. (1991). *Assessing higher order thinking and communication skills: Literacy.* Washington, DC: Natonal Center for Education Statistics (ERIC Document Reproduction Service No. ED 340 766)

This paper was commissioned by the U.S. Department of Education as background for a study design workshop for a national assessment of college student learning held in November 1991. The author addresses the task of defining literacy, the range of skills to be assessed, and the probability of assessing higher-order literacy skills separate from particular contexts. He also offers suggestions for the development of assessment tasks. Included are the comments of three reviewers. (ERIC) BI, CD, NT, OA, PR

285. Vroeijenstijn, A. I. (1995). *Improvement and accountability: Navigating between Scylla and Charybdis: Guide for external quality assessment in higher education* (Higher Education Policy Series 30). Bristol, PA: Jessica Kingsley. 188 pp.

This review of the assessment of quality in higher education discusses the reasons for interest in quality today, external quality assessment, performance indicators, assessment at various levels in an institution, funding, relationships with government, improvement versus accountability, basic principles, designing an assessment system, maintaining the integrity of the assessors, guidelines for self-study and external review committees, European systems of quality assessment, and national plans for the external assessment of institutions. Seven appendices provide a description of the Dutch university system, a checklist and formats for various reports and activities, a description of a means of faculty assessment, and an outline of the Dutch university quality assessment system for research. AY, BI, EE, FA, IT, IW, MT, NT, PI, RS, SC, U

286. Vroeijenstijn, A. I. (1995). Government and university: Opponents or allies in quality assurance? *Higher Education Review, 27*(3), 18-36.

Using as an example the experience of government policy for accountability and quality assurance in the Netherlands, the author discusses numerous aspects of government policy and institutional response and offers suggestions to ensure that assessment activities can be mutually productive for both the need of government for assurance of quality and institutions for improvement of quality. AY, GN, IT, TC, U

287. Wagenaar, Theodore C. (1995). Student evaluation of teaching: Some cautions and suggestions. *Teaching Sociology, 23*(1), 64-68.

This paper summarizes common misconceptions about student evaluations of instruction, common uses of these evaluations by colleges and universities, findings of research on rating forms, and problems with uses of these evaluations. The author explores the nature of effective instruction and recommends ways to improve the evaluation of instruction, among them to develop measures of learning toward clearly defined curricular outcome goals. The author offers to send readers "a comprehensive summary of the literature on student evaluation of teaching and a list of references" and "copies of commercial student evaluation forms and forms for peer and self-evaluation" (p. 64). EI, IN, PA, PR, TC, U

288. Wallace, John. (1985). *What undergraduates learn: The role of assessment in large research universities.* Paper presented at the AAHE Conference on Assessment in Higher Education, Columbia, South Carolina. (ERIC Document Reproduction Service No. ED 260 679) 18 pp.

This paper critiques educational processes in large research universities and considers what can be useful for thinking about assessment in all types of institutions. OA, RU

289. Warren, Jonathan R. (1971). *College grading practices: An overview* (Report 9). Washington, DC: ERIC Clearinghouse on Higher Education. (ERIC Document Reproduction Service ED 047 164) 29 pp.

This comprehensive review of the literature on grading practices includes grading effectiveness, systems, purposes, unintended effects, technical issues, and possible future directions. FR, GR, RR,

290. Warren, Jonathan R. (Ed.). (1983). *Meeting the new demand for standards.* New Directions for Higher Education, No. 43. San Francisco: Jossey-Bass. 101 pp.

This book reviews issues related to the increasing pressure from outside the academy for accountability. Included are accreditation; state concerns for student learning; problems relating to standards of time, content, expectations, cooperation, and ethics in American higher education; assessing classroom quality; the need for comprehensive examinations to separate teaching and learning from certification; the role of administrators in ensuring excellence; and contributions of the book to administrators. AR, AY, CE, ET, OA, SW

291. Warren, Jonathan. (1992). Learning as an indicator of educational quality. *Studies in Higher Education, 17*(3), 337-348.

The author reviews reasons for concern about the quality of undergraduate student learning in British and American colleges and universities, including the lack of useful data about learning and the limitations of grades and grade-point averages as indicators of learning. He describes the system of external examiners in the United Kingdom and a method of categorical grading that could improve the quality of evidence on students' learning in college. EE, EX, GR, IN, OA

292. Wergin, Jon F., & Braskamp, Larry A. (Eds.). (1987). *Evaluating administrative services and programs.* New Directions for Institutional Research, No. 56. San Francisco: Jossey-Bass. 105 pp.

Nine chapters by various authors discuss the context of evaluation and provide specific suggestions for evaluation of institutional planning, business offices, intercollegiate athletics, student support services, counseling centers, faculty development centers, and computing services. A final chapter by the editors discusses how to make the process of evaluation more useful. AD, D, FD, G, PA, PL, TH, U

293. White, Edward M. (1985). *Teaching and assessing writing: Recent advances in understanding, evaluating, and improving student performance.* San Francisco: Jossey-Bass. 304 pp.

The author reveals ways to develop writing assignments, teach revision, respond to student writing, measure writing ability, and use tests and other means of assessment as part of the writing process. Included are examples of ways to design valid and reliable writing tests, multiple methods of scoring writing, and an example of a writing course, including assignments, scoring guides, and sample student papers. P, PE, RB, W

294. White, Edward M. (1991). *Assessing higher order thinking and communication skills in college graduates through writing.* Washington, DC: National Center for Education Statistics. (ERIC Document Reproduction Service No. ED 340 767)

This paper was commissioned by the U.S. Department of Education as background for a study design workshop for a national assessment of college student learning held in November 1991. The author discusses the validity and reliability and effect on instruction of three methods of assessing writing: multiple-choice tests, essay examinations, and portfolios. He concludes that "any national assessment of writing should be principally or wholly a portfolio assessment." Included are comments by three reviewers. (ERIC) BI, CD, CT, NT, OA, PR, TC, W

295. White, Edward M. (1994). *Teaching and assessing writing: Recent advances in understanding, evaluating, and improving student performance.* (2nd ed.). San Francisco: Jossey-Bass. 331 pp.

The author draws on new knowledge about assessment to offer methods of evaluation and feedback. He shows how the use of assessment by teachers can assist the process of learning to write. In addition to outlining recent advances in teaching and assessing writing, the author explains how teachers can design writing assignments, help students write, and respond constructively to student writing. He includes a full discussion of the three most popular methods of assessing writing: multiple-choice tests, essay tests, and writing portfolios. P, PE, RB, W

296. Whiteley, Meredith A. (Ed.). (1992). *The primer for institutional research: Resources for institutional research, number seven.* Tallahassee, FL: Association for Institutional Research. 150 pp.

This handbook contains 11 chapters by various authors dealing with basic issues of institutional research: persistence, enrollment management, student impact, faculty demand, faculty salaries, peer institutions, diversity, environmental scanning, total quality management, academic program review, and cost analysis. Each chapter includes background discussion, literature, data analysis and communication, and a summary. (ERIC) (Also see Muffo and McLaughlin, 1987.) CQ, FI, IA, IC, IR, OA, PE

297. Williams, John H. (1990). Assessment, the affordable way. In Robert H. Woodroof (Ed.), *The viability of the private junior college.* New Directions for Community Colleges, No. 69 (pp. 33-42). San Francisco: Jossey-Bass.

This chapter is a general review of the use of outcome assessment in and value to small, private colleges. AY, CC, IW, LA, OA

298. Winona State University. (n. d.). *Mission and goals, quality assurance and assessment plan, long range plan.* Winona, MN: Winona State University. 40 pp.

These planning and assessment documents of Winona State University include the University's mission statement and general and specific process goals; principles and guidelines for assessment; input, process, and outcome goals, objectives, and indicators; quality enhancement matrix and long range plan, including vision statements for graduating students, faculty, staff, and administration; curriculum; graduate education; student development; facilities, space, and equipment; and relationship with the surrounding communities. Appendices include a description of the process used to develop components of the document, assumptions about the University's external and internal environment, the Minnesota State University System quality vision, six principles for campus life from the Carnegie report by that title, and the University's Quality Enhancement Matrix. CQ, CS, EX, G, IA, IN, IW, MG, MS, O, OA, OP, PA, PL, SP, SR, VS

299. Winston, Roger B., Jr., & Miller, Theodore K. (1994). A model for assessing developmental outcomes related to student affairs programs and services. *NASPA Journal, 32,* 2-19.

The authors introduce the importance of outcomes assessment of college students. They stress institutional mission in identifying outcomes to be measured and present several outcome taxonomies. A proposed model includes a ten-step approach to a comprehensive assessment program that is interactive, cyclical, and integrated. The model can be used at divisional or departmental levels, although institutional outcome assessment is thought to be ideal. The conclusion identifies potential political land mines. D, IS, IW, MS, MT, OA, SN

300. Witkin, Belle Ruth. (1984). *Assessing needs in educational and social programs.* San Francisco: Jossey-Bass. 415 pp.

This is a basic discussion for planners, evaluators, policy makers, and others concerned with assessing organizational needs. Included are relating needs assessment to program planning and evaluation; choosing the best needs-assessment model; gathering data; setting priorities, improving planning, and communicating information; facilitating use of results; cooperating across agencies; using needs assessment for community programs and services; and identifying implications for needs assessment in education, health, and human services. BI, MT, NA, PE, PL, SC, TH, U

301. Wolff, Ralph A. (1992). Incorporating assessment into the practice of accreditation: A preliminary report. In *Accreditation, assessment and institutional effectiveness: Resource papers for the COPA Task Force on Institutional Effectiveness* (pp. 19-36). Washington, DC: Council on Postsecondary Accreditation.

This article describes a survey of 15 accrediting bodies recognized by COPA concerning the role assessment played in their organizations. Questions concerned the knowledge and experience with assessment of association staff, their standards and guidelines on assessment, the amount of assessment training provided for campus visit team members, ways their institutions treated assessment in their self-studies, the role of assessment in team visits, actions taken by their higher education commissions concerning assessment results, and their personal views about assessment. The author analyses the results of the survey and offers eight conclusions. The survey instrument and tabulated responses follow the article, including open-ended responses to questions regarding barriers to and motivation toward assessment in member institutions and in agencies. AR, IS, IW, OA

302. Woodard, Dudley B., Jr., Hyman, Randy E., von Destinon, Mark, & Jamison, Alton. (1991). *Student affairs and outcomes assessment: A national survey.* NASPA Journal, 29, 17-23.

To determine the status of student outcomes assessment initiatives across the country, the authors surveyed the 1140 member institutions of the National Association of Student Personnel Administrators, using a paper and pencil instrument. Results indicate that 40% of the institutions had an assessment program, 21.2% were developing one, and 59.8% did not have and were not planning one. These and other results indicated that statewide initiatives influenced many of the plans at public institutions, student affairs professionals are involved in developing an outcomes assessment program, and a particular committee or officer directed most institutional outcomes assessment programs. After information on regional breakdown, source of support, and institution size, the authors conclude that "cooperative institutional collaboration involving faculty as well as academic and student affairs professionals" is the best response to the "apparent need for systematic programs to assess the knowledge, skills, and attitudes acquired by undergraduate students" (p. 22). IW, OA, SN, SW, U

303. Working Party on Effective State Action to Improve Undergraduate Education. (1986). *Transforming the state role in undergraduate education: Time for a different view* (No. PS-86-3). Denver, CO: Education Commission of the States. 40 pp.

This ECS report outlines eight problems in American undergraduate higher education and 22 recommendations to state higher education leaders for state action to improve undergraduate education. Included are a number of recommendations concerning assessment. AY, RR, SW

304. Yancey, Bernard D. (Ed.). (1988). *Applying statistics in institutional research.* New Directions for Institutional Research, No. 58. San Francisco: Jossey-Bass. 114 pp.

The editor and eight other authors discuss the relevance of classical experimental design to institutional research problems. Elements include continuous data when comparing groups, log-linear models, regression analysis, causal modeling (path analysis and linear structural relations—LISREL), forecasting methods, and exploratory data analysis methods. IR, ST, TH

305. Yarbrough, Donald B. (1992, Spring). Some lessons to be learned from a decade of general education outcomes assessment with the ACT COMP measures. *Innovative Higher Education, 16*(3), 223-234.

The author reviews the literature on the use of the ACT COMP Composite Exam and Objective Test. Based on his review, he evaluates the validity and reliability of these tests of cognitive education outcomes, reviews available information on student motivation, and discusses involving faculty in the process and evaluating for program improvement. GE, IS, MO, OA, TC, U, VA

306. Yelon, Stephen L., & Duley, John S. (1978). *Efficient evaluation of individual performance in field placement.* East Lansing, MI: Michigan State University. 28 pp.

This booklet, cosponsored by the Council for the Advancement of Experiential Learning (CAEL), helps coordinators and supervisors of student field experiences develop systematic, effective, and efficient evaluations of student performance. (For source see Davis and Alexander, 1977.) C, OA

Associations and Organizations

A number of institutions and organizations disseminate information about or provide training in assessment and evaluation. The following compilation of associations includes material from *Assessment Research, Evaluation, and Grading in Higher Education: Overview and Selected Resources* with permission from Lion F. Gardiner and from the *Encyclopedia of Associations* and the *Research Centers Directory* with permission from Gale Research.

Where applicable, the Web page of the organization is included. Some organizations also sponsor conferences and/or publish useful materials.

ACCREDITING ASSOCIATIONS

National

Council for Higher Education Accreditation (CHEA)
One Dupont Circle
Washington, DC 20036-1110
ph. (202) 955-6126
fax (202) 955-6129
e-mail: *chea@chea.org*
http://www.chea.org

The Council for Higher Education Accreditation (CHEA) serves students and their families, colleges and universities, sponsoring bodies, governments, and employers by promoting academic quality through formal recognition of higher education accrediting bodies. It coordinates and works to advance self-regulation through accreditation.

Regional

All six US regional higher education accrediting associations incorporate within their reaccreditation process an examination of institutions' outcomes. In addition to contact information (Web and e-mail where available) examples of references produced by regional associations for use in self-study prior to site visits are included.

Middle States Association of Colleges and Schools (MSA)
Commission on Higher Education
DE, DC, MD, NJ, NY, PA, Puerto Rico, Virgin Islands
3624 Market Street
Philadelphia, PA 19104
ph. (215) 662-5606
fax (215) 662-5501
Jean Morse, Executive Director
e-mail: *jmorse@aol.com*
http://www.webness.net/msa/

1996 & Beyond: Annual Report (1996)
Framework for Outcomes Assessment (1996)
Outcomes Assessment in the Middle States Region: A Report on the 1995 Outcomes Assessment Survey (July 1996)
Commission on Higher Education Newsletter (on-going)

New England Association of Colleges and Schools
Commission on Institutions of Higher Education
CT, ME, MA, NH, RI, VT
209 Burlington Road
Bedford, MA 01730-1433
ph. (617) 271-0022
fax (617) 271-0950
Vincent Ferrandino, Executive Director, *vferrandino@neasc.org*
e-mail: *cihe@neasc.org*
http://www.neasc.org

See the publications link on the Association web site for ordering information. Materials such as *Standards for Accreditation, Self-Study Guides,* and *Questions about Colleges and Universities* are available from the Commission on Institutions of Higher Education.

North Central Association of Colleges and Schools
Commission on Institutions of Higher Education
AZ, AR, CO, IA, IL, IN, KS, MI, MN, MO, NE, NM, ND, OH, OK, SD, WV, WI, WY
30 North LaSalle Street, Suite 2400
Chicago, IL 60602
ph. (800) 621-7440
fax (312) 263-7462
Steven D. Crow, Executive Director
e-mail: *info@ncacihe.org*
http://www.ncacihe.org

A Handbook of Accreditation, 1994-1996
Revised Sections of the Handbook of Accreditation (Criteria III & IV)
A Collection of Papers on Self-Study and Institutional Improvement (1996, 1995, 1994, 1993, 1992)
NCA Quarterly (on-going)
 Of particular interest are the following volumes:
 "Accreditation and Values in Higher Education" (Fall 1992)
 "Assessing Student Academic Achievement" (Fall 1992)
 "Sharpening the Focus on Assessment: The Regional and the NCA States" (Fall 1990)

Northwest Association of Schools and Colleges
Commission on Colleges
AK, ID, MT, NV, OR, UT, WA
3700-B University Way, NE
Seattle, WA 98105
ph. (206) 827-2005
fax (206) 685-4621
Sandra E. Elman, Executive Director

Directory of Accredited Postsecondary Institutions (1997)
Accreditation Handbook (1996)

Southern Association of Colleges and Schools
Commission on Colleges
AL, FL, GA, KY, LA, MS, NC, SC, TN, TX, VA
1866 Southern Lane
Decatur, GA 30033-4097
ph. (404) 679-4500
fax (404) 679-4558
James T. Rogers, Executive Director
(web page in progress)

Criteria for Accreditation (1996 with 1997 Addendum)
Resource Manual on Institutional Effectiveness (1996)
Handbook for Institutional Self-Study (1994)
Handbook for Peer Evaluators (1993)
Handbook for Committee Chairs (1992)

Western Association of Schools and Colleges
Senior College Commission and Accrediting Commission for Community and Junior Colleges (ACCJC)
CA, HI, American Samoa, Guam, Commonwealth of the Northern Marianas, and the Trust Territory of the Pacific Islands
c/o Mills College, Box 9990
Oakland, CA 94613-0990
ph. (510) 632-5000
fax (510) 632-8361
Ralph A. Wolff, Executive Director
http://www.wascweb.org

Handbook on Accreditation and Policy Manual (1996)
The Guide to Institutional Self-Study & Reports to the Commission (1996)
The Handbook for Evaluators (1991)

Specialized Accreditors

American Academy for Liberal Education (AALE)
Jeffrey D. Wallin
President
1015 Eighteenth Street, NW, Suite 204
Washington, DC 20036
ph. (202) 452-8611
fax (202) 452-8620

AALE was recognized in 1995 as an institutional and programmatic accreditor which focuses on liberal education as it is expressed through an institution's general education requirements and the Academy's own Education Standards, and is particularly interested in maintaining and improving teaching at member institutions.

Association of Specialized and Professional Accreditors (ASPA)
c/o Cynthia Davenport
Executive Director
1020 West Byron St., Suite 8G
Chicago, IL 60613-2987
ph. (773) 525-2160
fax (773) 525-2162
e-mail: aspacd@aol.com

ASPA represents the interests of the specialized and professional accreditation community to higher education and to government. It provides a forum for those who wish to improve accreditation. It conducts research, develops analyses, and both makes and recommends policy. Membership in ASPA is linked to the member Code of Good Practice; a copy of the Code is available from the ASPA Office. The membership roster includes representatives from the accrediting bodies of the following disciplines: Allied Health, Acupuncture, Architecture, Art and Design, Business, Chiropractic, Clinical Laboratory Science, Computer Sciences, Construction, Counseling, Dance, Dentistry, Dietetics, Engineering, Family and Consumer Science, Forestry, Health Services Administration, Interior Design, Journalism, Landscape Architecture, Library and Information Studies, Marriage and Family Therapy, Music, Nuclear Medicine, Nurse Anesthesia, Nursing, Occupational Therapy, Optometry, Pharmacy, Physical Therapy, Podiatry, Psychology, Public Health, Public Affairs, Radiologic Technology, Recreation and Parks, Rehabilitation Counseling, Speech-Language-Hearing, Teacher Education, and Theatre.

HIGHER EDUCATION ASSOCIATIONS

For a list of web pages for over 150 associations, see
http://www.apollo.gmu/~jmilam/air95/assoc.html

American Association for Higher Education (AAHE)
One Dupont Circle, Suite 360
Washington, DC 20036-1110
ph. (202) 293-6440
fax (202) 293-0073
http://www.aahe.org

The American Association for Higher Education (AAHE) is a national organization of more than 8,500 individuals dedicated to improving the quality of higher education. AAHE members share two convictions: that higher education should play a more central role in national life and that each of our institutions can be more effective. AAHE helps to translate those convictions into action through its programmatic activities, publications, and conferences. The Assessment Forum, a project of AAHE, is the primary national network connecting and supporting higher education stakeholders involved in assessment. It promotes thoughtful, effective approaches to assessment that involve faculty, benefit students, and improve the quality of teaching and learning, and sponsors an annual Conference on Assessment &

Quality. For a list of assessment publications from AAHE, including commissioned papers from the 1993, 1994, and 1995 conferences and the often cited "Principles for Good Practice for Assessing Student Learning," see *http://www.aahe.org/publist3.htm#Pubs-Assessment.*

American Educational Research Association (AERA)

1230 17th St., N.W.
Washington, DC 20036
ph. (202) 223-9485
fax (202) 775-1824
http://aera.net

AERA is an association of educators and behavioral scientists interested in the development, application, and improvement of educational research. Members include professors, state and local school system research directors, research specialists, graduate students of education, and educators in foreign countries. Division J is the group of AERA members whose focus is postsecondary educational research.

American Evaluation Association (AEA)

UNC 1 Greensboro
Greensboro, NC 27412-5001
ph. (910) 334-4095
fax (910) 334-5882
http://www.eval.org

AEA membership includes individuals from university, government, research, consulting, corporate education, and industrial research settings who represent various disciplines including psychology, education, public administration, marketing, social work, and policy analysis. AEA works to improve evaluation theory, practice, training programs, professional competencies, and evaluation utilization. Activities include compilation of a directory of training programs in evaluation, support for professional standards for evaluation, review of federal support for evaluation research, and the study of evaluation in particular settings.

Association of American Colleges and Universities (AAC&U)

1818 R St., N.W.
Washington, DC 20009
ph. (202) 387-3760
fax (202) 265-9532
http://www.aacu-edu.org

AAC&U membership includes colleges and universities, that "are committed to promoting humane and liberating learning." The association offers practical advice to aid colleges and universities in developing effective academic programs and improving curricula and services. While focusing on quality undergraduate education, AAC&U seeks to improve public understanding of the value of a liberal education by conducting research and providing consultation services on curriculum, assessment, and institutional management issues.

Association for Institutional Research (AIR)

Florida State University
314 Stone Bldg.
Tallahassee, FL 32306-3038
ph. (904) 644-4470
fax (904) 644-8824
http://www.fsu.edu/~air/home.htm

Membership in AIR includes individuals interested in institutional research or policy analysis in the improvement of planning, management, and resource allocation. AIR fosters research leading to improved understanding, planning, and operation of institutions of postsecondary education. The association encourages the application of appropriate methodologies and techniques and publishes and exchanges information concerning institutions of higher learning. AIR also offers an electronic newsletter to its members.

Association for the Study of Higher Education (ASHE)

Dept. of Educational Administration
Texas A&M University
College Station, TX 77843-4226
ph. (409) 845-0393
fax (409) 862-4347
http://www.coe.missouri.edu/~ashe

The purposes of ASHE are to advance the study of higher education and facilitate and encourage discussion of priority issues for research in the study of higher education. Members include professors, researchers, administrators, policy analysts, graduate students, and others concerned with the study of higher education. Note that as of January 1998, the ASHE Secretariat will be located at the University of Missouri-Columbia (e-mail: *ashe@tiger.coe.missouri.edu*).

Education Commission of the States (ECS)

707 17th St., Suite 2700
Denver, CO 80202-3427
ph. (303) 299-3692
fax (303) 296-8332
http://www.ecs.org

The Education Commission of the States (ECS) is a nonprofit, nationwide compact formed in 1965 to help governors, state legislators, state education officials, and others develop policies to improve the quality of public education at all levels. ECS sponsors an annual meeting and forum which often addresses assessment issues.

For a list of over 40 research centers, see
http://apollo.gmu.edu/~jmilam/air95/centers.html.

Center for Postsecondary Research and Planning
School of Education, 4228
201 N. Rose Ave.
Indiana University
Bloomington, IN 47405-1006
ph. (812) 856-8364
fax (812) 856-8394
e-mail: *hesa@indiana.edu*
http://www.indiana.edu/~cseq

The Center exists to provide services to federal, state, and institutional policy planners and administrators in both public and private colleges and universities. Center associates address policy issues that include student persistence and attrition, institutional advancement, enrollment management, and institutional culture. The Center also manages the College Student Experiences Questionnaire (CSEQ) Research and Distribution Program.

ERIC Clearinghouse on Assessment and Evaluation
Catholic University of America
210 O'Boyle Hall
Washington, DC 20064
ph. 800-GO4-ERIC
or (202) 673-3811
fax (202) 319-6692
e-mail: *eric_ae@cua.edu*
http://ericae2.educ.cua.edu/main.htm

The Clearinghouse on Assessment and Evaluation seeks to provide resources to encourage responsible test use. The scope of articles indexed includes methodology of measurement research and evaluation, applications of tests, measurement or evaluation in educational projects or programs, research design and methodology in the area of assessment and evaluation, and learning theory. ERIC serves the community by answering user questions, performing searches for users interested in educational assessment and evaluation related topics, acquiring new documents for inclusion in the ERIC database, and providing access to documents. In addition to a database of over 10,000 test descriptions, the award winning web site includes a subject matter directory on assessment, a cross site search engine, databases of full text resources and journal article abstracts, and more.

ERIC Clearinghouse on Community Colleges (ERIC/CC)
UCLA
3051 Moore Hall
Box 951521
Los Angeles, CA 90095-1521
ph. (800) 832-8256
or (310) 825-3931
fax (310) 206-8095
e-mail: *ericcc@ucla.edu*
http://www.gse.ucla.edu/ERIC/eric.html

ERIC/CC provides searches of the ERIC database on community college-related topics, assistance in developing search strategies and conducting bibliographic research, assistance in locating ERIC microfiche collections, workshops on using ERIC, and general information. ERIC/CC also provides an opportunity for those involved in community college education to become partners of the Clearinghouse.

ERIC Clearinghouse on Higher Education (ERIC/HE)
One Dupont Circle, Suite 630
Washington, DC 20036
ph. (800) 773-3742
or (202) 296-2597
fax (202) 296-8379
http://www.gwu.edu/~eriche

The ERIC Clearinghouse is known nationally and internationally as a center for information about higher education, including assessment. The Clearinghouse concentrates on education beyond the secondary level leading to a four-year, master's or professional degree (see also ERIC Clearinghouse on Community Colleges). The range of information includes students, faculty, graduate and professional education, legal issues, financing, planning and evaluation, curriculum, teaching methods, and state-federal-institutional questions. The ERIC Clearinghouse on Higher Education offers help in constructing ERIC database searches and has reference bibliographies available; acts as a consultant for individuals; and provides users, through a web site with greater access to information.

ASHE-ERIC Publications concerning assessment include: *Successful Faculty Development and Teaching: The Complete Portfolio* (95-8), *Benchmarking in Higher Education: Adapting Best Practices to Improve Quality* (95-5), *Redesigning Higher Education: Producing Dramatic Gains in Student Learning* (94-7), *Student Goals for College and Courses: A Missing Link in Assessing and Improving Academic Achievement* (89-6), *and College Student Outcomes Assessment: A Talent Development Perspective* (87-7). For a catalog/order form, contact the Clearinghouse.

Higher Education Research Institute (HERI)
UCLA Graduate School of Education
Los Angeles, CA 90024
ph. (310) 825-1925
fax (310) 206-2228
http://www.gse.ucla.edu/heri/heri.html

HERI conducts research on higher education institutions, federal and state policy assessment, minority access to higher education, student and faculty development, retention, women's issues, leadership, and values in higher education. HERI also conducts the Annual Survey of American College Freshmen (CIRP) in which survey data is collected on 280,000 freshmen from 600 institutions each fall. Follow-up surveys are conducted every three years. National faculty surveys are conducted every three years.

National Center for Higher Education Management Systems (NCHEMS)
P.O. Box 9752
Boulder, CO 80301-9752
ph. (303) 497-0301
fax (303) 497-0338
e-mail: *nchems@colorado.edu*
http://www.nchems.com

NCHEMS has since 1969 been devoted to research, development, education, and direct assistance aimed at improving management in higher education. NCHEMS serves colleges, universities, state-level agencies, national and regional associations, and other research, development, and service organizations. Among its other activities, NCHEMS has been involved in studies of college outcomes and outcome assessment. The web site includes detailed information about publications on assessment and survey research available through NCHEMS.

National Center for Postsecondary Improvement (NCPI)
Project on Student Learning and Assessment
610 E. University, Room 2339
University of Michigan
Ann Arbor, MI 48109-1259
ph. (313) 647-7768
fax (313) 936-2741

Headed by Michael Nettles of the Center for the Study of Higher and Postsecondary Education at the University of Michigan, this project examines postsecondary assessment and its impact on teaching and learning. The Project on Student Learning and Assessment represents an innovative attempt to examine state policy, institutional-level assessment, and faculty/student perspectives as vital components of one continuous system.

Documents available from this project include *Charting Higher Education Assessment: An Analysis of State and Accreditation Association Policies and Practices, A Research Agenda for Institutional Support for Enhancing Student Assessment and Performance: A Literature Review,* and *A Review of National Data for Understanding Teaching, Learning, and Assessment in Postsecondary Institutions.* In addition, one website for part of the project is available: *http://www-personal.umich.edu/~mmatney/NCPI/contents.html.*

National Center on Postsecondary Teaching, Learning, and Assessment (NCTLA) at the Center for the Study of Higher Education
403 South Allen St., Suite 104
Pennsylvania State University
University Park, PA 16801-5252
ph. (814) 865-1738
fax (814) 865-3638
e-mail: *NCTLA@psuvm.psu.edu*
http://www.psu.edu/research/irp/cshe/info/research/nc.html

NCTLA is a research, development, and dissemination center that seeks to discover what facilitates student learning. NCTLA is comprised of faculty members, administrators, and researchers at Penn State, the University of Illinois at Chicago, Syracuse University, Northwestern University, Arizona State University, and the University of Southern California. Occasional assessment institutes and workshops are sponsored by NCTLA, some in cooperation with other associations such as AAHE, ACT, NASPA, and NCHEMS.

The Center for the Study of Higher Education engages policy analysis of major trends, issues, and practices in higher education at the institutional, state, regional, and national levels. Specific research initiatives include postsecondary teaching, learning assessment, program review and evaluation, the impact of college on students, strategic and regional planning, organizational cultures, business-industry relationships with colleges and universities, and international higher education.

NONPROFIT TESTING COMPANIES

ACT
David A. Lutz
Director, ACT Postsecondary Services
2201 North Dodge Street, P.O. Box 168
Iowa City, IA 52243-0168
ph. (319) 337-1000 (general)
or (319) 337-1053 (Postsecondary Programs & Services)
fax (3190 337-1790
e-mail: *lutz@act.org*
http://www.act.org

ACT, a nonprofit educational-services organization, is a pioneer in outcomes assessment. Its expertise in measuring student outcomes dates to the 1970s and the College Outcome Measures Program (COMP), which includes six instruments for assessing general education. ACT has since developed additional related assessment systems:

the Collegiate Assessment of Academic Proficiency (CAAP), with six instruments to measure foundational academic skills; the Critical Thinking Assessment Battery, for measuring the reasoning and communicating outcomes of college; and Work Keys, with eight instruments for assessing workplace skills. Hundreds of institutions have used one or more of these programs to assess thousands of students, yielding an extensive database and numerous research reports. ACT also offers a range of surveys for obtaining opinion feedback from students and alumni and numerous models for helping institutions develop successful assessment processes. ACT offers free publications concerning institutions assessing outcomes. These include "College Assessment Planning," "Increasing Student Competence and Persistence," "Postsecondary Measures of Reasoning and Critical Thinking," and "Report of ACT's Research on Postsecondary Assessment Needs."

ETS

Carol Owen
Program Administrator
ETS Higher Education Assessment
Educational Testing Service
Rosedale Road (55-L)
Princeton, NJ 08541-0001
ph. (609) 921-9000
fax (609) 683-2270
e-mail: cowen@ets.org
http://www.ets.org

ETS Higher Education Assessment (HEA) offers a broad range of tests, questionnaires, and other instruments as well as support staff to provide faculty members and administrators with information and services essential for informed decision making. HEA can help institutions developing programs of assessment to improve educational programs. The Academic Profile (jointly sponsored with the College Board) measures college-level reading, writing, mathematics, and critical thinking in the context of material from the humanities, social sciences, and natural sciences. Institutional Assessment Questionnaires are available to assess graduate programs and evaluate educational objectives (Goals Inventories), and to provide feedback on the teaching and learning environment (Student Instructional Reports). ETS also offers Major Field Tests that measure the academic abilities and achievement of undergraduate students as they complete coursework in their majors, and Tasks in Critical Thinking (TASKS), a performance-based assessment of critical thinking stills.

Alverno College
3401 South 39th Street, P.O. Box 343922
Milwaukee, WI 53234-3922
ph. (414) 382-6087
fax (414) 382-6354
http://www.alverno.edu

Alverno College, widely known for its outcome-based curriculum, publishes materials available to other institutions and individual faculty members (see http://www.alverno.edu/educator/epublic.htm). Alverno also sponsors on-campus assessment workshops and institutes.

Assessment Resource Center
2800 Maguire Blvd.
University of Missouri-Columbia
Columbia, MO 65211
ph. (800) 366-8232
e-mail: arctpars@muccmail.missouri.edu
http://www.tiger.coe.missouri.edu/~arcwww/arc.html

The Assessment Resource Center offers comprehensive assessment assistance to individuals and to institutions in areas including research and evaluation, test and survey development, hand-scoring of performance assessments, statistical analyses, and interpretation and reporting.

New England Assessment Network
Bernard Gill
North Shore Community College
One Ferncroft Road, P.O. Box 3340
Danvers, MA 01923-0840
ph. (508) 762-4000, ext. 5420
e-mail: bjg@shore.net

This network acts as a way for faculty and administrators in the New England area to share information and resources. Established in 1995, the New England Assessment Network holds two conferences per academic year.

New Mexico Higher Education Assessment Directors
Dr. Fred Lillibridge
Assistant Provost for Institutional Effectiveness
NMSU Alamogordo
P.O. Box 477
Alamogordo, New Mexico 88311
ph. (505) 439-3624
fax (505) 439-3643
e-mail: flillibr@nmsuvm1.nmsu.edu

The New Mexico Higher Education Assessment Directors networking association sponsors an annual assessment conference and publishes H.E.A.D.line, a semi-annual newsletter. To see on-line versions of recent issues, see http://www.enmu.edu/~testaa/headlines.

North Carolina Assessment Network
The North Carolina Assessment Network is unique in that conversations are conducted on-line. Annual assessment meetings are also sponsored by the Network.

The moderated listserver, established in November 1996, includes faculty members, staff, and administrators from public and private four-year institutions and community colleges in the state. It provides broad-based participatory involvement in discussions of assessment, both inside and outside the classroom.

For questions about the list, send e-mail to the list owner at *owner-ncassessnet@ncccs.cc.nc.us.*

To subscribe to the list, send e-mail to *majordomo@ncccs.cc.nc.us.* In the body of the message, enter only: *subscribe ncassessnet.*

Office of Planning and Institutional Improvement

Trudy W. Banta
Vice Chancellor
Office of Planning and Institutional Improvement
Indiana University Purdue University Indianapolis
355 N. Lansing, AO 140
Indianapolis, IN 46202-2896
ph. (317) 274-4111
fax (317) 274-4651
e-mail: *tbanta@iupui.edu*
http://www.hoosiers.iupui.edu/paiimain/paiimain.htm

Trudy W. Banta and her staff have compiled annotated bibliographies and other documents: Selected Resources on Assessment and Improvement, Annotated Bibliography: Works from a Decade of Outcomes Assessment in Higher Education (1985-1995), and Articles on the Assessment of Student Learning from *Assessment Update,* Volumes 1-6 (1989-1994). For information about ordering these documents, contact the Office of Planning and Institutional Improvement.

Portland State University Center for Academic Excellence

Amy Driscoll
Director
P.O. Box 751-CAE
Portland, OR 97207-0751
ph. (503) 725-5642
fax (503) 725-5262
e-mail: *driscoll@po.pdx.edu*

The Center for Academic Excellence provides support for faculty in their teaching, assessment, and community-university partnerships. The support takes the form of workshops and seminars, technical assistance, resource library, and mentoring.

An example of a publication available from the Center is *Assessing the Impact of Service Learning: A Workbook of Strategies and Methods.* This comprehensive guide assists faculty, students, institutional leaders and community partners in understanding and assessing the impact of community-based service learning. The workbook includes an overview of assessment strategies, a series of assessment measures, guides for the administration of each measure, and suggestions for how to use assessment data to further improve teaching and learning. To purchase the workbook, contact the Center for Academic Excellence.

South Carolina Higher Education Assessment Network

Marge Tebo-Messina
SCHEA Network
210 Tillman Hall
Winthrop College
Rock Hill, SC 29733
ph. (803) 323-2341
fax (803) 323-2359
e-mail: *tebomessinam@winthrop.edu*

The South Carolina Higher Education Assessment (SCHEA) Network is a voluntary consortium of over 45 colleges, universities, and higher education agencies working together to establish high quality institutional effectiveness assessment efforts and foster quality improvement among its members. SCHEA sponsors a fall conference and spring assessment seminars.

The SCHEA Network Annotated Bibliography (1990) includes sections on assessment of general education, college readiness, career preparation, personal growth and development, assessment of majors and specialty areas, retention, and minority students. Also included are bibliographies about theoretical aspects of assessment, data analysis and interpretation, and survey research. To purchase a copy of this bibliography, contact the SCHEA Network.

Virginia Assessment Group (VAG)

Carmon Kiah, Ph.D.
John Tyler Community College
13101 Jefferson Davis Highway
Chester, VA 23831
ph. (804) 796-4012
fax (804) 796-4163
http://www.jmu.edu/vag/

The Virginia Assessment Group (VAG) is an association of college personnel engaged in institutional assessment activities on their respective campuses. VAG is dedicated to the goals of promoting the continued high quality of higher education in the Commonwealth of Virginia through assessment practices. VAG serves as a forum for the expression of ideas about assessment practices and as a network for communication and collaboration among public and private institutions and state agencies. VAG also sponsors an annual assessment conference.

STUDENT AFFAIRS ASSOCIATIONS

American College Personnel Association (ACPA)
One Dupont Circle, N.W., Suite 300
Washington, DC 20036-1110
ph. (202) 835-2272
fax (202) 296-3286
http://www.acpa.nche.edu

Members of ACPA are employed in higher education and involved in student personnel work, including administration, counseling, research, and teaching. The organization fosters student development and learning in higher education in areas of service, advocacy, and standards by offering professional programs for educators committed to the overall development of postsecondary students. ACPA sponsors professional and educational activities in cooperation with other organizations.

National Association of Student Personnel Administrators (NASPA)
1875 Connecticut Ave. NW, Suite 418
Washington, DC 20009
ph. (202) 265-7500
fax (202) 797-1157
http://www.naspa.org

NASPA works to enrich the educational experience of all students. It serves colleges and universities by providing leadership and professional growth opportunities for the chief student affairs officer and other professionals who consider higher education and student affairs issues from an institutional perspective. It provides professional development, improves information and research, and acts as an advocate for students in higher education. NASPA promotes diversity within its members and in the profession.

Conferences

Information about assessment conferences was compiled from Assessment Forum files, *The Chronicle of Higher Education*, a national assessment listserv, and other Internet resources. Specific dates are listed when available; if not, general meeting dates are indicated. In addition, regional associations and members of the Association of Specialized and Professional Accreditors (ASPA) often hold assessment meetings and symposia. Please contact the regional associations directly for information. ASPA (see p. 64 of Association section) can provide specific contact information. Note special indication (*) of sponsoring organizations described elsewhere in this resource guide.

AAHE Annual Conference on Assessment & Quality
dates: June each year
American Association for Higher Education (AAHE) *
One Dupont Circle, Suite 360
Washington, DC 20036
ph. (202) 293-6440
fax (202) 293-0073
e-mail: *assess@aahe.org*
http://www.aahe.org

This annual conference is the premiere national and international gathering of assessment practitioners and policymakers. Each year since 1985, more than 1,200 faculty members, administrators, researchers, and other higher education stakeholders have met in June to learn and share the latest developments in assessment. Novices, veterans, and experts focus on issues of assessment and quality improvement, connecting assessment practice with application of quality improvement to academic work.

American Evaluation Association Annual Meeting
dates: fall each year
American Evaluation Association (AEA) *
ph. (910) 334-4095
fax (910) 334-5882
http://www.theriver.com/public/aea

This annual conference is sponsored by AEA, an international professional association of evaluators devoted to the application and exploration of program evaluation, personnel evaluation, technology, and many other forms of evaluation. AEA has a topical interest group on Assessment in Higher Education.

Annual Alverno College Assessment Seminars and Workshops
dates: various
Alverno College Institute *
3401 S. 39th Street, PO Box 343922
Milwaukee, WI 53234-3922
ph. (414) 382-6087
fax (414) 382-6354
http://www.alverno.edu

Alverno College conducts various once-a-year seminars for educators. In November and April one-day seminars entitled A Day at Alverno College: Teaching and Assessing Student Abilities are offered to faculty and administrators and a two-day workshop is offered for nursing educators. In June, Alverno conducts two concurrent week-long workshops: Assessment-as-Learning: Teaching and Assessing Student, Program and Institution; and Teaching for Outcomes: A New Look at the Disciplines.

Annual ASHE Conference
dates: November each year
Association for the Study of Higher Education (ASHE) *
Dept. of Educational Administration
Texas A&M University
College Station, TX 77843-4226
ph. (409) 845-0393
fax (409) 862-4347
e-mail: *bjones@acs.tamu.edu*
http://www.coe.missouri.edu/~ashe

This annual conference serves professors, researchers, administrators, policy analysts, graduate students, and others concerned with the study of higher education. Areas of interest include the teaching-learning process, students, and policy development. Note that as of January 1998, the ASHE Secretariat will be located at the University of Missouri-Columbia (e-mail: *ashe@tiger.coe.missouri.edu*).

Annual International Conference on Assessing Quality in Higher Education
dates: mid-July each year
IUPUI in association with H+E Associates, U.K.
355 N. Lansing, AO 140
Indianapolis, IN 46202
ph. (317) 274-4111
fax (317) 274-4651
e-mail: *tbanta@iupui.edu*
http://www.hoosiers.iupui.edu/paiimain/conferen.htm

The purposes of this conference series are to promote awareness of current issues and perspectives on the assessment of quality in higher education world-wide and to provide presentations by leading exponents of a variety of perspectives designed to promote cross-cultural discussion and interaction.

*See Associations and Organizations

Annual Summer Institute for Institutional Effectiveness and Student Success

dates: June each year
Consortium for Community College Development
2030M School of Education
610 E. University
Ann Arbor, MI 48109-1259
ph. (313) 647-1978
fax (313) 647-6911
e-mail: cccd@umich.edu
http://www.umich.edu/~cccd

Community college professionals from across the United States and Canada learn about innovative models, programs, and practices related to the improvement of institutional performance and student success. The Summer Institute's philosophy is collaborative and programmatic.

Annual Virginia Assessment Group Conference

dates: November each year (November 5-7, 1997)
Virginia Assessment Group *
College of William & Mary
Williamsburg, VA 23187-8795
ph. (757) 221-3584
fax (757) 221-2390
e-mail: slbosw@facstaff.wm.edu
http://www.jmu.edu/vag/vagevent.html

This professional forum promotes practical aspects of assessment as applied in the Commonwealth of Virginia. The Conference includes presentations on assessment practices that work, and addresses current and future issues in institutional, state, and national assessment policies and practices. Participants include faculty members, administrators, students, assessment practitioners, and others involved in assessment-related activities in higher education.

Assessment Conference in Indianapolis

dates: early to mid-November each year
IUPUI
355 N. Lansing, AO 140
Indianapolis, IN 46202
ph. (317) 274-4111
fax (317) 274-4651
e-mail: tbanta@iupui.edu
http://www.hoosiers.iupui.edu/paiimain/conferen.htm

This conference provides a context for exchanging information with colleagues who have first-hand knowledge of assessment. Continuing sub-themes include assessment in general education and the academic major. Past conferences have focused on assessment in health professions and in business fields and on the use of technology in assessment.

*See Associations and Organizations

Colloquium on Writing Assessment

dates: October each year
Missouri Colloquium on Writing Assessment
Longview Community College
500 SW Longview Road
Lee's Summit, MO 64081-2105
ph. (816) 672-2529
fax (816) 672-2078
e-mail: grahn@longview.cc.mo.us
http://www.mwsc.edu/~cwa

This conference is sponsored by the Missouri Colloquium on Writing Assessment for writing professionals from Missouri two-year and four-year institutions of higher learning who are active and/or interested in writing assessment research and projects.

Colorado Regional Assessment Conference

dates: annual conference
Colorado Association of Higher Education
Assessment Directors
c/o Norine Domenico
16000 E. Centre Tech Parkway
Aurora, CO 80011-9036
ph. (303) 360-4778
fax (303) 360-4761
e-mail: ca_norine@mash.colorado.edu

This annual conference draws participants from Colorado and neighboring states. Sponsored by an informal network of assessment directors, the organizer and location of this conference change each year. For information about each year's conference theme and dates, contact Norine Domenico and watch the ASSESS listserv (see p. 90).

ECS National Forum & Annual Meeting

dates: July each year
Education Commission of the States (ECS) *
707 17th St., Suite 2700
Denver, CO 80202-3427
ph. (303) 299-3600
fax (303) 296-8332
e-mail: ecs@ecs.org
http://www.ecs.org

This conference is an annual meeting of governors, state and local policy makers, and those working to improve the quality of education at all levels (elementary through higher education).

International Congress on the Assessment Center Method

dates: each year (May 11-14, 1998 in Pittsburgh, PA; June 1-4, 1999, in Orlando, FL; May 2000 in Washington, DC)
Development Dimensions International
1225 Washington Pike
Bridgeville, PA 15017-2838
ph. (800) 933-4463
fax (412) 257-3916
e-mail: cnelson@ddiworld.com
http://www.ddiworld.com

This annual conference provides a forum for sharing new technology, research of assessment methodologies, and case studies of assessment centers throughout the world.

Middle States Outcomes Assessment Symposia

dates: various
Middle States Commission on Higher Education *
3624 Market Street
Philadelphia, PA 19104
ph. (215) 662-5606, ext.17
fax (215) 662-5501
http://www.webness.net/msa

This continuing series for faculty, academic administrators, and institutional researchers at colleges and universities in the Middle States region addresses assessment issues. Topics include steps in developing a plan; ways that assessment outcomes can improve teaching, learning, and institutional effectiveness; and ways to present the case for outcome assessment.

Midwestern Conference on Performance Assessment

dates: spring each year
Center for Learning, Evaluation, and Assessment Research
CLEAR, 5 Hill Hall
University of Missouri-Columbia
Columbia, MO 65211
ph. (573) 882-0987
fax (573) 882-0768
e-mail: cthomas@tiger.coe.missouri.edu
http://tiger.coe.missouri.edu/~clear

This conference focuses on performance assessment in both K-12 and higher education. Practitioners, policy makers, and researchers at all educational levels present sessions and panels. Previous conference themes have focused on assessment policy, research, and reform, and standards-based education.

National Institute on Assessment of Experiential Learning

dates: June each year
Thomas Edison State College
101 W. State Street
Trenton, NJ 08608-1176
ph. (609) 633-8082
fax (609) 777-2957
e-mail: ddagavarian@call.tesc.edu
http://www.tesc.edu

This conference is an intensive learning experience designed for professionals in education. Beginning and advanced tracks are available to accommodate participants with different levels of experience in prior learning assessment.

NCTLA/ACT Assessment Institutes

dates: various
National Center on Postsecondary Teaching, Learning, and Assessment (NCTLA) * and ACT *
403 South Allen St., Suite 104
University Park, PA 16801-5252
ph. (814) 865-5917
fax (814) 865-3638
e-mail: nctla@psuvm.psu.edu
http://www.psu.edu/research/irp/cshe/

By applying the latest research, NCTLA/ACT institutes help prepare participants for accrediting visits and aid in increasing communication with community leaders, statewide agencies, and accrediting agencies. Faculty work with institutions to develop, implement, or enhance their assessment plans in order to enrich student learning, create a more coherent and effective curriculum, improve student advising, increase faculty development activities, and provide documentation of student achievement.

New England Assessment Forum

dates: April each year
New England Assessment Network *
Bernard Gill
North Shore Community College
One Ferncroft Road, P.O. Box 3340
Danvers, MA 01923-0840
ph. (508) 762-4000, ext. 5420
e-mail: bjg@shore.net

This network acts as a way for faculty and administrators in the New England area to share information and resources. Established in 1995, the New England Assessment Network holds two conferences per academic year.

New Mexico Higher Education Assessment Conference

dates: February each year
New Mexico Higher Education Assessment Association *
Dr. Fred Lillibridge
P.O. Box 477
NMSU Alamagordo
Alamagordo, NM 88311
ph. (505) 439-3624
fax (505) 439-3643
e-mail: flillibr@nmsuvm1.nmsu.edu
http://www.nmsu.edu/~NMAC97/

This conference, designed and developed by local practitioners, highlights assessment experiences at New Mexico's higher education institutions. Conference participants learn how similar institutions have addressed outcome assessment, share their own experiences, and discover instruments and tools available from national publishers.

Northumbria Assessment Conference

dates: September each year
Educational Development Service
University of Northumbria at Newcastle
Newcastle Upon Tyne, NE3 SNY, ENGLAND
ph. 44 191 227 4180
fax 44 191 227 3985
e-mail: m.dickson@unn.ac.uk
http://www.unn.ac.uk/~edu8/assessconf.html

This international conference focuses on assessment of student learning in colleges and universities. The 1997 conference theme is "Encouraging Partnership in Assessing Learners."

*See Associations and Organizations

South Carolina Higher Education Assessment Conference
dates: November each year (November 13-15, 1997)
South Carolina Higher Education Assessment (SCHEA)
Network *
210 Tillman Hall, Winthrop University
Rock Hill, SC 29733
ph. (803) 323-2341
fax (803) 323-2359
e-mail: tebomessinam@winthrop.edu

This conference provides an annual opportunity for exchange of assessment information among postsecondary educators from across the state and nation.

Student Learning Institute
dates: May each year
Box 3501
James Madison University
Harrisonburg, VA 22801
ph. (540) 568-6597
fax (540) 568-6719
e-mail: wardwl@jmu.edu

The Institute is a concentrated opportunity for student affairs practitioners, faculty members, academic administrators, graduate students, and others to learn how to create, manage, and assess learning environments on the college or university campus. Topics include building faculty-student affairs partnerships, assessing student learning outcomes, becoming a learning organization, measuring the impact of experiential learning, and many others.

Texas Assessment Conference
dates: February each year
Texas Association of School Administrators
(cosponsors with Texas Association of Collegiate
Testing Personnel, National Association of Test Directors,
and Texas Education Agency)
406 E. 11th Street
Austin, TX 78701-2617
ph. (512) 477-6361
fax (512) 482-8658
http://www.tasanet.org

This conference is the only statewide conference in Texas specifically dedicated to assessment and testing in education. The conference brings together teachers, counselors, school administrators, college-level instructors, and testing specialists, and members of the TEA staff and the Texas Higher Education Coordinating Board. Conference topics cover a broad spectrum of assessment issues that cross K-12 and higher education settings.

*See Associations and Organizations

The Association for Institutional Research Annual Forum
dates: May each year (May 17-20, 1998;
May 30-June 2, 1999)
The Association for Institutional Research (AIR)
Florida State University
114 Stone Building
Tallahassee, FL 32306-3038
ph. (904) 644-4470
fax (904) 644-8824
e-mail: air@mailer.fsu.edu
http://www.fsu.edu/~air/home.htm

This national meeting of institutional researchers offers over 200 contributed papers, panels, and demonstrations including an International Symposium. Two of the seven component tracks are Institutional Effectiveness, Student Learning, and Outcomes Assessment and Enrollment Management and Student Affairs.

Using Cases & Classroom Assessment to Improve Teaching and Learning
dates: summer each year (August 9-13, 1997;
July 16-20, 1998)
Pace University
861 Bedford Road
Pleasantville, NY 10570-2799
ph. (914) 773-3879
fax (914) 773-3878
e-mail: silverma@pace.edu

This small working conference draws college faculty interested in using case teaching and classroom assessment to improve student learning and active participation. Held annually on the University of British Columbia campus in Vancouver, the conference urges participants to be actively involved in their learning.

Washington State Higher Education Assessment Conference
dates: May each year (May 13-15, 1998;
May 12-14, 1999)
State Board for Community and Technical Colleges
PO Box 42495
Olympia, WA 98504
ph. (360) 753-3676
fax (360) 586-0050
e-mail: mcneill_anna/SBCTC@ctc.edu

This annual conference on assessment in higher education is designed for two- and four-year faculty and administrators. Although the vast majority of participants are from Washington, participants from neighboring states are welcome.

Instruments

This section is reprinted with permission from *Assessment 101 Workbook* by Michael K. Smith and Jama L. Bradley. *Assessment 101: A Video Guide to Designing and Implementing an Assessment Program* (1995, video and workbook) is available for purchase from the authors {call (800) 743-1574, or e-mail *michaelks@aol.com*}. The AAHE Assessment Forum has not added or updated entries and has not examined instruments listed in this section. The Forum has updated the contact information to include phone, fax, e-mail, and internet addresses where possible.

This section is made up of three parts: General Information, a Timeframe Matrix, and instruments to assess Competencies. The timeframe matrix developed by Smith and Bradley classifies assessment instruments according to students' status: entering students, continuing students, withdrawing students, graduating students, and alumni. Within each category are examples of instruments that assess basic skills, general education, knowledge of the major, student experiences, and institutional effectiveness. The final two parts of the matrix address two competencies that are frequently assessed: critical thinking and writing.

GENERAL INFORMATION

ERIC/AE Test Locator, a very thorough web site, can be found at *http://www.ericae2.educ.cua.edu/testscol.htm*. This site includes the capability to search the Educational Testing Service (ETS) Test File, a Test Review Locator, and the Buros/ERIC Test Publisher Locator. At the Clearinghouse site there is also a list of Test Selection Tips.

The following three sources provide additional information about student affairs instruments.

The ACPA Commission IX-Assessment for Student Development Clearinghouse on Environmental and Student Development Assessment Instruments is maintained on-line at *http://www-isu.indstate.edu/dragon/ix-indx.html*. This database includes descriptions and reviews of instruments and is indexed by subject, title, and author (see Internet section).

In *Assessment in Student Affairs: A Guide for Practitioners,* Schuh and Upcraft (1996) include an appendix (pp. 325-344) with Assessment Instrument Annotations. The book is also the foundation for an Assessment in Student Affairs Workshop (workshop notebooks available from NCTLA at CSHE, The Pennsylvania State University, 403 South Allen Street, Suite 104, University Park, PA 16801-5252, ph. (814) 865-5917, fax (814) 865-3638). Contact M. Lee Upcraft at CSHE address for information about continuing updates (see Association section for NCTLA; see Assessment Library for an abstract of *Assessment in Student Affairs*).

Student Affairs-Related Outcomes Instruments: Summary Information. (Spring 1994; Joint project of the Student Affairs Division and the Office of Institutional Research and Planning, University of Texas-Arlington; partially funded by a research grant from the Texas Association of College and University Student Personnel Administrators). This monograph includes an overview of student affairs assessment and detailed information, including reliability and validity data, about a number of instruments. For a copy of the monograph, contact Sam Stigall, Office of Institutional Research and Planning, ph. (817) 272-3132; or Linda S. Moxley, Student Affairs Division, ph. (817) 272-5375.

Addresses

Included in this section are multiple tests from the following companies. The addresses are listed here and referred to later.

ACT
2201 North Dodge Street
P.O. Box 168
Iowa City, IA 52243-1068
ph. (319) 337-1053
fax (319) 337-1790
e-mail: *lutz@act.org*
http://www.act.org

Alverno College
3401 South 39th Street
Milwaukee, WI 53234-3922
ph. (414) 382-6087
fax (414) 382-6354
http://www.alverno.edu

ETS
Rosedale Road
Princeton, NJ 08541
ph. (609) 921-9000
fax (609) 683-2270
http://www.ets.org

NCHEMS
1540 30th Street
P.O. Drawer P
Boulder, CO 80302
ph. (303) 497-0301
fax (303) 497-0338
e-mail: *nchems@colorado.edu*
http//www.nchems.com

TIMEFRAME MATRIX

Entering Students
BASIC SKILLS

ACCUPLACER-Computerized Placement Tests (CPT)
ETS

Computerized placement tests can be administered using microcomputers. Area tests include reading comprehension, arithmetic, writing, algebra, sentence skills, and mathematics. ETS recognizes over 115 institutions who have used or are using the ACCUPLACER. Reliability and normative data are available.

ACT Assessment
ACT

ACT Assessment can be used in measuring basic skills, providing baseline data for institutional research, and predicting academic performance. Reliability, validity, and other statistical data are available from ACT.

ACT ASSET Program
ACT

Basic and Advanced Skill (ability profile) Assessment are part of this program, which also includes instruments to evaluate study skills, career skills, Entering Student Report, and Returning Student Report. Statistical and reporting information is available from ACT.

Alverno College Assessment Instruments
Alverno College

Assessments for Entering Students in reading, writing, speaking, listening, computer literacy, and quantitative literacy are available.

Assessment and Placement Services for Community Colleges
ETS

Designed by the College Board specifically for community colleges, this battery of assessment instruments can assess areas of reading, writing, and mathematics. It includes an optional essay component, student placement inventory, and placement research service.

Comprehensive Test of Basic Skills (CTBS)
CTB McMillan/McGraw-Hill
2500 Garden Road
Del Monte Research Park
Monterey, CA 93940
ph. (800) 538-9547
fax (800) 282-0266
http://www.ctb.com

CTBS consists of up to ten subject areas used to assess basic skills. They are vocabulary, reading comprehension, spelling, language mechanics, language expressions, mathematics computation, mathematics concepts and applications, reference skills, science, and social studies. Technical data are available.

Scholastic Aptitude Test (SAT)
SAT/ETS
P. O. Box 6736
Princeton, NJ 08541
ph. (609) 771-7600
http://www.ets.org
(see also *http://www.collegeboard.org*)

The SAT was designed for use as a college entrance and placement examination. The SAT is comprised of two tests, verbal and quantitative. Research findings indicate that both test scores on the SAT are related to college performance during the first two years.

Test of Adult Basic Education (TABE)
CTB McGraw-Hill
Del Monte Research Park
2500 Garden Road
Monterey, CA 93940
ph. (800) 538-9547
fax (800) 282-0266
http://www.ctb.com/adult.htm

TABE is used to place students in adult education programs. Subject areas include vocabulary, comprehension, mathematics computations, mathematics concepts and applications, language mechanics, language expression, and spelling. Information on norms and criterion-reference are available from CTB/McGraw-Hill.

The Council for Adult and Experiential Learning (CAEL)
CAEL
243 S. Wabash Ave., Suite 800
Chicago, IL 60604
ph. (312) 922-5909
fax (312) 922-1769
http://www.cael.org

CAEL provides guidance, information, and assessment programs for adult and experiential learning. CAEL procedures evaluate credit for learning outside the classroom and for life experiences.

STUDENT EXPERIENCES

Entering-Student Questionnaire, 2-year and 4-year versions
NCHEMS

The survey is designed to gain information from entering students.

Entering Student Survey
ACT

This survey collects information related to students' plans, goals, and impressions at the time they enter college. This instrument requires approximately 20 minutes to complete and contains the following five sections: Background information (15 items), Educational Plans and Preferences (60 items), College Impressions (62 items), Additional Questions (up to 30 items), and Comments and Suggestions.

The Retention Management System
Noel-Levitz Centers, Inc.
Noel-Levitz Office Park
2101 ACT Circle
Iowa City, Iowa 52245-9581
ph. (319) 337-4700
or (800) 876-1117
fax (319) 337-5274
http://www.usagroup.com/noelevtz/main.htm

These materials identify students with high drop-out tendencies and target those likely to be receptive to help, estimate potential for academic difficulty, appraise various dimensions of a student's academic motivation, and identify tendencies toward educational stress.

Continuing Students
BASIC SKILLS

College Level Academic Skills Test (CLAST)
Florida Department of Education
Student Assessment Services Section
Turlington Building, Suite 414
Tallahassee, Florida 32399-0400
ph. (904) 488-8198
fax (904) 488-1627
http://www.firn.edu/doe/sas/sasshome.htm

CLAST was developed as part of an overall effort by the state of Florida to ensure that students have achieved the communication and computation skills expected of college sophomores. Areas covered by the CLAST include reading, writing, computation, and an essay.

GENERAL EDUCATION

The Academic Profile (AP)
ETS Higher Education Assessment Services

The AP was developed to assist in assessing outcomes of general education programs to improve the quality of instruction and learning. Nine subject areas may be covered. An optional essay component comes with directions on how to score essays. AP is available in short and long form. Reliability and validity information, as well as norm and criterion-referenced scores, are available from ETS.

Alverno College Assessment Instruments
Alverno College Assessment Council

College Basic Academic Subjects Examination (CBASE)
The Riverside Publishing Company
425 Spring Lake Drive
Itasca, IL 60143
ph. (800) 323-9540
fax (630) 467-7192
http://www.hmco.com/hmco/riverside

The CBASE is intended to assess content knowledge and skill development at a level commensurate with students completing the general education component of college or near the end of the sophomore year. The instrument tests knowledge in four subject areas and can include a writing sample. The CBASE is criterion referenced.

Collegiate Assessment of Academic Proficiency (CAAP)
ACT

The focus of the CAAP is the assessment of general education foundation skills typically attained in the first two years of college. CAAP offers two options to measure writing skills: a written skills test or a writing essay test. Other areas include reading, science reasoning, mathematics and critical thinking. Statistical information is available upon request.

Education Assessment Series (EAS)
ETS

EAS tests are modifications of the CLEP exams and are designed to provide information about student outcomes for program evaluation. The series consists of two tests intended to provide comprehensive nationally normed data in a relatively short administration time and at a low cost. An essay option is available with the English Composition exam; however, it is scored by the institution.

University of Connecticut-General Education Assessment
General Education Assessment Project
University of Connecticut
28 North Eagleville Road
Storrs, CT 06269-3135
ph. (860) 486-3879
fax (860) 486-1909
http://www.uconn.edu

The University of Connecticut project consists of assessment in six general education goal areas. It contains 16 instruments used for general education assessment at the University of Connecticut.

Portfolio Assessment of General Education
Lendley Black
College of Liberal Arts and Sciences, Box 4010
Emporia State University
Emporia, KS 66801
ph. (316) 341-5278
fax (316) 341-5681
e-mail: *blacklen@esumail.emporia.edu*
http://www.emporia.edu/S/www/asem/dept.htm

KNOWLEDGE OF THE MAJOR

ACT Proficiency Examination Program: Earth Science
ACT

This objective test is designed to allow credit by examination.

Advanced Placement Program Examinations
ETS

These examinations cover materials in full-year introductory college courses with similar titles. Most examinations take three hours. They are used for placement in advanced courses. Comparative data are available.

College Level Examination Program (CLEP) General Education Examinations
ETS

The CLEP offers curriculum-related, institutionally administered examinations in English composition, American history, business, computers, data processing, foreign languages, management, marketing, accounting, micro and macro economics, trigonometry, western civilization and mathematics for the assessment of general education outcomes. Reference data for entering freshmen and end-of-year sophomores are available from EAS. Statistical data are also available.

DANTES: History of Western Civilization to 1500
ETS

This test is designed to allow college credit by course equivalency.

STUDENT EXPERIENCES

ACT Student Opinion Survey, 2-year and 4-year versions
ACT, Evaluation/Survey Services

The purpose of this instrument is to explore the perceptions of enrolled students.

College Student Experiences Questionnaire (CSEQ)
CSEQ
Center for Postsecondary Research & Planning
School of Education #4228
201 North Rose Avenue
Indiana University
Bloomington, IN 47405-1006
ph. (812) 856-8041
fax (812) 856-8394
e-mail: *cseq@indiana.edu*
http://www.indiana.edu/~cseq

This questionnaire is designed to measure student experiences and involvement within the college environment.

Community College Student Experiences Questionnaire (CCSEQ)
Patricia Murrell
Center for the Study of Higher Education
100 Education Annex 1
University of Memphis
Memphis, TN 38152
ph. (901) 678-2775
fax (901) 678-4257
e-mail: *murrellp@cc.memphis.edu*
http://www.coe.memphis.edu/coe/CSHE/cshe.html

This questionnaire is designed to measure student experiences and involvement within the community college environment.

Continuing-Student Questionnaire 2-year and 4-year versions
NCHEMS

This survey is part of a comprehensive series provided by NCHEMS and is designed to survey continuing students.

Quality & Importance of Recreational Services Survey

NIRSA
850 SW 15th Street
Corvallis, OR 97333
ph. (541) 737-2088
fax (541) 737-2026
e-mail: *nirsa@proaxis.com*
http://nirsa.org

This survey was developed in 1991 by the Center for Assessment Research & Development in conjunction with the National Intramural Recreational Sports Association. The survey and technical manual were specifically developed to assess student development outcomes associated with student services in general and recreational sports in particular.

The Student Satisfaction Inventory

Noel-Levitz Centers, Inc.
Noel-Levitz Office Park
2101 ACT Circle
Iowa City, Iowa 52245-9581
ph. (319) 337-4700
or (800) 876-1117
fax (319) 337-5274
http://www.usagroup.com/noelevitz/main.htm

This inventory provides information regarding the aspects of campus life that students consider most and least important as well as measures of student satisfaction.

The University Residence Environmental Scale

Mindgarden
P.O. Box 60669
Palo Alto, CA 94306
ph. (415) 424-8493
or (415) 424-0475
http://www.mindgarden.com

The University Residence Environment Scale was designed to assess the social climate of university student living groups, such as residence halls, fraternities, sororities, and cooperative residence units.

INSTITUTIONAL EFFECTIVENESS

Academic Freedom Survey

Jeannette Heritage
Psychometric Affiliates
Box 807
Murfreesboro, TN 37133-0807
ph. (615) 898-2565
fax (615) 898-5027

This survey was designed by the Academic Freedom Committee of the Illinois Division, American Civil Liberties Union. It measures the extent to which rights of students, teachers, and others are effectively assured in an institutional setting.

College and University Classroom Environment Inventory (CUCEI)

Professor Barry J. Fraser, Director
Science and Mathematics Education Center
Western Australian Institute of Technology
Kent Street
Bentley, Western Australia 6102

This inventory was developed to assess student and teacher perceptions of various dimensions of the actual and preferred environment. The CUCEI is available from ERIC Document Reproduction Services, 7420 Fullerton Road, Suite 110, Springfield, VA 22153-2852. (ED 274 692, 25 pages)

Institutional Performance Survey

NCHEMS

This survey intends to assess how various institutional conditions are related to an institution's external environment, strategic competence, and effectiveness.

Institutional Student Survey-Truman State University

Nancy Asher
Office of Assessment and Testing
East Normal Street
Truman State University
Kirksville, MO 63501-0828
ph. (816) 785-4228

Instructor/Course Evaluation Form

Bethany Lutheran College
734 Marsh Street
Mankato, MN 56001-4490
ph. (507) 386-5326
fax (507) 386-5376

Resource Guide for Assessing Campus Climate

California Postsecondary Education Commission Publications
1303 J Street, Suite 500
Sacramento, CA 95814
ph. (916) 322-8024
fax (916) 327-4417
http://www.cpec.ca.gov

This two-part guide results from a three-year study by the CPSEC on the feasibility of developing an educational equity assessment system designed to obtain information on the perceptions of institutional participants about their campus climate. Part One illustrates how colleges and universities throughout California have used a variety of methods in assessing facets of their campus climate. Part Two contains three pools of items—students, faculty, and staff—that institutions can use to design surveys of campus climate. Also available are Assessing Campus Climate: Feasibility of Developing an Educational Equity Assessment System, and Toward an Understanding of Campus Climate.

University of Virginia School of Education Course Evaluation Form
Dr. Linda Bunker
Curry School of Education
University of Virginia
Charlottesville, VA 22903-2495
ph. (804) 924-0740
fax (804) 924-0888
e-mail: *lbunker@virginia.edu*
http://Curry.edschool.virginia.edu

Student Instructional Report (SIR)
ETS

This report is a brief, objective questionnaire designed to aid in evaluating and improving instruction and faculty development.

Student Outcomes Information Services (SOIS)
NCHEMS

SOIS is a complete evaluation system for assessment from entering freshmen to alumni information.

Toward an Understanding of Campus Climate
Office of Assessment
Jacksonville State University
700 Pelham Road North
Jacksonville, AL 36265
ph. (205) 782-5109
fax (205) 782-5149
e-mail: *tasmith@jsucc.jsu.edu*

This is a survey of campus climate and cultural diversity.

Withdrawing Students
STUDENT EXPERIENCES

Former-Student Questionnaire, 2-year and 4-year versions
NCHEMS

This instrument is part of a comprehensive series and is designed to survey students who withdraw.

The University of Tennessee Retention Survey (The Student Experience at UTK-A Look Back)
The Institute for Assessment and Evaluation
312 Claxton Education Building
University of Tennessee
Knoxville, Tennessee 37996-3400
ph. (423) 974-6800
fax (423) 974-6848

The survey was designed to be used with student dropouts or stopouts.

Withdrawing/Nonreturning Student Survey
ACT

This survey is designed to determine the reasons students leave an institution prior to completing a degree or certification program. This instrument requires approximately 20 minutes to complete and contains the following five sections: Background Information (16 items), Reasons for Leaving College (48 items), College Services and Characteristics (46 items), Additional Items (up to 30 items), and Comments and Suggestions.

Graduating Students
GENERAL EDUCATION

The Academic Profile (AP)
ETS Higher Education Assessment Services

The AP was developed to assist in assessing outcomes of general education programs to improve the quality of instruction and learning. Nine subject areas may be covered. An optional essay component comes with directions on how to score essays. AP is available in short and long form. Reliability and validity information, as well as norm and criterion-referenced scores, are available from ETS.

Alverno College Assessment Instruments
Alverno College Assessment Council

College Outcome Measures Program (COMP)
ACT

The COMP is designed to assess higher order cognitive skills using realistic problems rather than discipline- or content-based outcomes. The COMP is organized in two dimensions, process and content, and offers six instruments. Data are used to assess general education proficiency, baseline data, and growth from entry to exit. Statistical data and reporting format are available from ACT.

University of Connecticut-General Education Assessment
General Education Assessment Project
University of Connecticut
28 North Eagleville Road
Storrs, CT 06269-3135
ph. (860) 486-3879
fax (8600 486-1909
http://www.uconn.edu

The University of Connecticut project consists of assessment in six general education goal areas. It contains 16 instruments.

Portfolio Assessment of General Education
Lendley Black
College of Liberal Arts and Sciences, Box 4010
Emporia State University
Emporia, KS 66801
ph. (316) 341-5278
fax (316) 341-5681
e-mail: *blacklen@esumail.emporia.edu*
http://www.emporia.edu/S/www/asem/dept.htm

PORTFOLIO ASSESSMENT OF GENERAL EDUCATION

Margaret Tebo-Messina
General Education Assessment
Winthrop University
Rock Hill, SC 29733
ph. (803) 323-2341
fax (803) 323-2359
e-mail: *tebomessinam@winthrop.edu*

KNOWLEDGE OF THE MAJOR

Area Concentration Achievement Tests (PACAT)
Anthony Golden
Project for Area Concentration Achievement Testing
Austin Peay State University
Box 4568
Clarksville, TN 37044
ph. (615) 648-7451
fax (615) 648-6127
e-mail: *pacat@apsu01.apsu.edu*
http://www.apsu.edu/~pacat

These tests are designed primarily for the evaluation of departmental curricula against a national sample of similar departments. Although individual students' scores can be obtained from the PACAT, they can be used only as general guides rather than absolute indicators of individual performance.

Graduate Record Examinations (GRE)
ETS Graduate Record Examinations Program

Although designed as an entrance exam for graduate programs, the GRE has been used by institutions as an exit examination. Verbal, quantitative, and analytical scores are available for the general examination. Specialty area exam scores are also available. The target population is college seniors who intend to attend graduate school, usually as they complete their major programs. The primary purpose of the subject area tests is ". . . to help the graduate school admission committees and fellowship sponsors assess the qualifications of applicants in their subject fields. The tests also provide students with a means of assessing their own qualifications. Scores on the tests are intended to indicate students' mastery of the subject matter emphasized in many undergraduate programs as preparation for graduate study." (GRE Subject Tests Descriptive Booklet, page 3.)

Major Field Tests
ETS Higher Education Assessment Services

These tests are designed to assess students' mastery of concepts, principles, and knowledge, as well as ability to analyze, solve problems, understand relationships, and interpret material as an outcome of study in a specific major. The tests are based on Graduate Record Examination Subject Tests, but are shortened and less difficult. They are appropriate for all seniors, not just those planning graduate study.

PORTFOLIO ASSESSMENT OF THE MAJOR

▶ ALL MAJORS (ALTERNATIVE ASSESSMENTS)

Assessment Resource Center
Roberta Mullen, Director
2800 Maguire Blvd.
University of Missouri-Columbia
Columbia, MO 65211
ph. (800) 366-8232
fax (5730 882-8937
http://tiger.coe.missouri.edu/~arcwww/main.htm

Alverno College
3401 South 39th Street
Milwaukee, WI 53234-3922
ph. (414) 382-6087
fax (414) 382-6354
http://www.alverno.edu

Kean College of New Jersey
Dr. Michael E. Knight
Morris Avenue
Union, NJ 07083
ph. (908) 527-2661
fax (908) 629-7222

Clearinghouse for Higher Education Assessment Instruments
312 Claxton Education Building
University of Tennessee
Knoxville, Tennessee 37996-3400
ph. (423) 974-6800
fax (423) 974-6878

▶ SOCIAL WORK

The University of Tennessee
Frank J. Spicuzza
204 Henson Hall
Knoxville, TN 37996
ph. (423) 974-3351
fax (423) 974-4803
e-mail: *fspicuzz@utk.edu*

STUDENT EXPERIENCES

Program-Completer and Graduating-Student Questionnaire
NCHEMS

Part of a series, this questionnaire is designed in 2-year and 4-year versions for senior students to assess students' experiences and opinions.

Program Self-Assessment Service (PSAS)
ETS Higher Education Programs

This service was developed to assist undergraduate departments in evaluating their programs.

College Student Needs Assessment Survey
ACT Evaluation/Survey Services

This survey is designed to assist college personnel in assessing the educational and personal needs of college students. This instrument requires approximately 20 minutes to complete. The College Student Needs Assessment Survey is organized into five sections: Background Information (14 items), Career and Life Goals (22 items), Educational and Personal Needs (59 items), Additional Questions (up to 30), and Comments and Suggestions.

Geneseo Annual Senior Survey
James L. McNally
Office of Institutional Research
Erwin 222
SUNY Geneseo
1 College Circle
Geneseo, NY 14454
ph. (716) 245-5553
fax (716) 245-5005
e-mail: mcnally@sgenaa.cc.geneseo.edu

This survey is designed to evaluate academic experiences.

Graduating Student Questionnaire, 2-year
Charles Houston
Director, Institutional Research and Planning
P.O. Box 14007
Virginia Western Community College
Roanoke, VA 24038
ph. (540) 857-7314
fax (540) 857-7544
e-mail: vhousc@vw.cc.va.us

The questionnaire is designed to survey students completing their program on the community college level.

Graduating Student Questionnaire-Truman State University
Nancy Asher
Office of Assessment and Testing
East Normal Street
Truman State University
Kirksville, MO 63501-0828
ph. (816) 785-4228

Marquette University Senior Survey
Dr. Mark D. McCarthy
Dean of Student Development
Alumni Memorial Union, Room 329
P.O. Box 1881
Milwaukee, WI 53201-1881
ph. (414) 288-1412
e-mail: MCCARTHYM@vms.csd.mu.edu

This instrument was developed to assess the development of students during their collegiate years and the relationship of development to involvement in student affairs programs and services.

Senior Transition Survey
Dr. Janet Schmidt
Director of Institutional Studies
University of Maryland at College Park
2119 Main Administration Building
College Park, MD 20742
ph. (301) 405-5596
fax (301) 314-9443
e-mail: jschmidt@umdacc.umd.edu

Supplemental Items for Seniors-University of Tennessee
The Institute for Assessment and Evaluation
312 Claxton Education Building
University of Tennessee
Knoxville, Tennessee 37996-3400
ph. (423) 974-6800
fax (423) 974-6848

INSTITUTIONAL EFFECTIVENESS

For descriptions of the following tests, see the Continuing Students Institutional Effectiveness section:

Academic Freedom Survey
Campus Community at Virginia Tech
Institutional Performance Survey
Institutional Self-Study-Truman State University
Resource Guide for Assessing Campus Climate
Toward an Understanding of Campus Climate

Graduate Program Self-Assessment Service
ETS

Alumni

ACT Alumni Outcomes Survey
ACT

The instrument is designed to obtain student satisfaction feedback and self-reported perceptions of growth in many areas considered important by accrediting commissions and other external agencies.

ACT Alumni Survey, 4-year college form
ACT

This instrument helps the 4-year institution evaluate the impact of the college on its graduates.

ACT Alumni Survey, 2-year college form

ACT

This survey helps the 2-year institution evaluate the impact of the college on its graduates. The instrument requires approximately 25 minutes to complete and contains the following seven sections: Background Information (12 items), Continuing Education (6 items), Educational Experiences (53 items), Employment History (29 items), Additional Questions (up to 30 items), Current Mailing Addresses (3 items), and Comments and Suggestions.

Alumni Survey-Truman State University

Nancy Asher
Office of Assessment and Testing
East Normal Street
Truman State University
Kirksville, MO 63501-0828
ph. (816) 785-4228

Bemidji State University-Alumni Survey

Dr. Linda Baer, Sr.
VP for Academic and Student Affairs
Bemidji State University
1500 Birchmont Drive
Bemidji, MN 56601
ph. (218) 755-2015
fax (218) 755-4048

This questionnaire is part of a comprehensive assessment plan. The alumni survey is used to gain insight on the present state and past experiences of alumni.

COFHE Alumni Survey

Consortium on Financing Higher Education
Suite 307
238 Main Street
Cambridge, MA 02142
ph. (617) 253-5030
fax (617) 258-8280

Comprehensive Alumni Assessment Survey (CAAS)

NCHEMS

CAAS is designed to be used with or without local questions, as well as to be a comprehensive tool for gathering information.

Five-year Alumni Survey

Dr. Donald Reichard
Office of Institutional Research
103 Forney Building
The University of North Carolina at Greensboro
Greensboro, NC 27412-5001
ph. (910) 334-5930
fax (910) 334-5932
e-mail: reichard@iris.uncg.edu

This survey obtains data on recent baccalaureate degree recipients with regard to employment and educational activities since receiving their baccalaureate degree.

Long-Term Alumni Questionnaire

NCHEMS

This instrument is designed to survey alumni who have been away from the institution more than four years.

Recent-Alumni Questionnaire

NCHEMS

This survey is designed to survey recent alumni.

Student Outcomes Information Services (SOIS)

NCHEMS

SOIS is a complete evaluation system from entering freshmen to alumni information.

COMPETENCIES

Critical Thinking/ Cognitive Development Skills

Adjective Check List

Consulting Psychologists Press
3803 E. Bayshore Road
P.O. Box 10096
Palo Alto, CA 94303
ph. (800) 624-1765
or (415) 969-8901
http://www.cpp-db.com

California Critical Thinking Dispositions Inventory

The California Academic Press
217 La Cruz Avenue
Milbrae, CA 94030
ph. (415) 697-5628
e-mail: info@calpress.com
http://www.calpress.com

This inventory is a psychological measure of seven critical thinking dispositions: truth-seeking, open-mindedness, analyticity, systematicity, self-confidence, inquisitiveness, and maturity.

California Critical Thinking Skills Test

The California Academic Press
217 La Cruz Avenue
Milbrae, CA 94030
ph. (415) 697-5628
e-mail: info@calpress.com
http://www.calpress.com/skill.html

This test assesses logical thinking ability targeting analysis, inference, and evaluation.

Learning Styles Inventory

TRG
Hay/McBer
116 Huntington Ave.
Boston, MA 02116
ph. (800) 729-8074
or (617) 437-7080
fax (617) 425-0073
e-mail: TRG_McBer@haygroup.com
http://www.haygroup.com

The Learning Styles Inventory is a widely used and applied instrument based on Kolb's Experiential Learning Theory. The self-scoring test can be completed and scored in less than 30 minutes. A bibliography and technical specifications are available upon request when the Learning Styles Inventory is ordered.

Cornell Critical Thinking Test

Critical Thinking Books and Software
P.O. Box 448
Pacific Grove, CA 93950
ph. (800) 458-4849
fax (408) 393-3277
e-mail: ct@criticalthinking.com
http://www.criticalthinking.com

This test assesses general critical thinking ability including induction, deduction, evaluation, observation, credibility (of statements made by others), assumption identification, and meaning.

Creative Reasoning Test (CRT)

Critical Thinking Books and Software
P.O. Box 448
Pacific Grove, CA 93950
ph. (800) 458-4849
fax (408) 393-3277
e-mail: ct@criticalthinking.com
http://www.criticalthinking.com

The CRT measures the ability to generate and evaluate problem solutions in a variety of categories.

Defining Issues Test

Center for the Study of Ethical Development
c/o James Rest
206A Burton Hall
University of Minnesota
178 Pillsbury Drive SE
Minneapolis, MN 55455
ph. (612) 624-6083
fax (612) 624-8241
http://www.coled.umn.edu/EdPsy/CSED/default.htm

The DIT is a measure of one aspect of moral development. It measures what factors one takes to be relevant to solving moral problems.

Dimensions of Self-Concept, College Form

Educational and Industrial Testing
P.O. Box 7234
San Diego, CA 92167
ph. (619) 222-1666
fax (619) 226-1666

This short, easy-to-administer instrument is designed to assess self-concept in a school setting.

Ennis-Weir Critical Thinking Essay Test

Critical Thinking Books and Software
P.O. Box 448
Pacific Grove, CA 93950
ph. (800) 458-4849
fax (408) 393-3277
e-mail: ct@criticalthinking.com
http://www.criticalthinking.com

The Ennis-Weir essay test measures various aspects of critical thinking. It is a test of a person's ability to critically evaluate an argument for a thesis. It requires the person to formulate, in writing, an evaluation of the argument and give reasons for the evaluation.

Erwin Scale of Intellectual Development

T. Dary Erwin
Developmental Analytics
P. O. Box 855
Harrisonburg, VA 22801

Establishment of identity is the core developmental vector in Arthur Chickering's theory. Identity is generally considered the answer to the question "Who am I?" The quest for personal identity is a major developmental task, particularly for traditional age college students. For Chickering, the concept of identity includes conceptions concerning body and appearance and clarification of sexual identification. Erwin added a third component to the definition of identity, that of personal confidence.

Logical Reasoning (1955)

Mindgarden
P.O. Box 60669
Palo Alto, CA 94306
ph. (415) 424-8493
or (415) 424-0475
http://www.mindgarden.com

The Logical Reasoning instrument measures the ability to evaluate semantic implications or the logical soundness of meaningful conclusions.

Measure of Epistemological Reflection (MER)

Marcia B. Baxter Magolda
Department of Educational Leadership
350 McGuffey Hall
Miami University
Oxford, OH 45056
ph. (513) 529-6837
fax (513) 529-1729
e-mail: mbbaxter@miamiu.muohio.edu

The purpose of the MER is to assess cognitive development using the Perry scheme. The instrument measures six domains of intellectual development.

Measure of Intellectual Development (MID)

William S. Moore
Coordinator
Center for the Study of Intellectual Development
1505 Farwell Ct. NW
Olympia, WA 98502
ph. (360) 786-5094
e-mail: wsmoore@earthlink.net

Created by Lee Knefelkamp and Carole Widick, the MID is a production-task measure using sentence stems and essay tasks. The instrument is designed to assess cognitive/intellectual developments as defined in the Perry scheme.

Myers-Briggs Type Indicator (MBTI)

Consulting Psychologists Press, Inc.
3803 E. Bayshore Road
P.O. Box 10096
Palo Alto, CA 94303
ph. (800) 624-1765
or (415) 969-8901
http://www.cpp-db.com

The MBTI is a personality assessment tool that measures a person's basic preferences for how they become aware or how they gather information, and how they draw conclusions or make decisions. The MBTI has been widely used as a measure of a student's learning style.

Parker Cognitive Development Inventory

Albert Hood
HITECH Press
P.O. Box 2341
Iowa City, IA 52244
ph. (319) 335-5278

Based on Perry's theory of cognitive development, this instrument is designed to yield an objectively scored measure of sequential and hierarchical developmental positions of cognitive development.

Problem Solving Inventory (PSI)

Consulting Psychologists Press, Inc.
3803 E. Bayshore Road
P.O. Box 10096
Palo Alto, CA 94303
ph. (800) 624-1765
or (415) 969-8901
http://www.cpp-db.com

The PSI measures how people react to everyday communication and types of personal problems (i.e., depression, inability to get along with friends, choosing a vocation, marital problems, etc.).

Reflective Judgement Interview (RJI)

Karen S. Kitchener and Patricia A. King
Department of Higher Education and Student Affairs
330 Education Building
Bowling Green State University
Bowling Green, OH 43403-0249
ph. (419) 372-7382
fax (419) 372-9382

The Reflective Judgement Interview was designed to assess the seven stages of Reflective Judgement model as outlined by Kitchener and King in 1981. The instrument is used to assess the student's stage level within the model.

Tasks in Critical Thinking (TASKS)

ETS Higher Education Assessment

TASKS uses an extended task format for performance-based assessment of critical thinking skills.

Tennessee Self-Concept Scale

Western Psychological Services
12031 Wilshire Blvd.
Los Angeles, CA 90025-1251
ph. (310) 478-2061
fax (310) 478-7838

The Tennessee Self-Concept Scale was designed to measure an individual's level of self-concept. Self-concept is defined as a set of perceptions and expectations about personal competencies, limitations, typical behavior, relationships with others, and feelings of positive or negative personal worth.

Watson-Glaser Critical Thinking Appraisal

The Psychological Corporation
555 Academic Court
San Antonio, TX 78204-2498
ph. (800) 211-8378
or (210) 299-1061
fax (800) 232-1223

The Watson-Glaser Critical Thinking Appraisal is a standardized test to measure various aspects of critical thinking. The CTA is composed of five subject areas: inference, recognition of assumptions, deduction, interpretation, and evaluation of arguments.

Writing Assessments

College English Placement Test (CEPT)

The Riverside Publishing Company
425 Spring Lake Drive
Itasca, IL 60143
ph. (800) 323-9540
fax (630) 467-7192
http://www.hmco.com/hmco/riverside

The test measures four areas of English: organization and paragraph structure, syntax and grammar, vocabulary development and diction, and usage and capitalization. CEPT provides information for student placement, indicates weaknesses in specific language areas, and provides insights bearing on the process of written composition. The test consists of a mandatory objective section and an optional essay section.

Developing a Multidisciplinary, Multimethod Approach to Writing Assessment
SCHEA Network
Winthrop University
Rock Hill, SC 29733
ph. (803) 323-2341
fax (803) 323-2359
e-mail: *tebomessinam@winthrop.edu*

Pre-Professional Skills Test of Reading, Mathematics, and Writing (PPST)
ETS Teaching and Learning Division

Sections of the PPST include reading, mathematics, writing test and essay. These tests are designed to measure basic proficiency in each area of teacher training. Statistical information is available from ETS.

Writing Proficiency Exam
Southeast Missouri State University
Writing Center, MS 4600
Cape Girardeau, MO 63701
ph. (573) 651-2159
fax (573) 986-6198

Believing that graduates should be competent writers, SMSU not only requires students to take freshman composition classes and to pass a writing proficiency test (WP003) after completing 75 hours of coursework. They must also take a writing test (WP002) upon completion of the required course in written expression.

BASIC SKILLS AND GENERAL EDUCATION INSTRUMENTS WITH OPTIONAL OR REQUIRED WRITING COMPONENTS:

Academic Profile
Assessment and Placement Services for
    Community Colleges
College Basic Academic Subjects Examination
College English Placement Test
College Level Academic Skills Test
Collegiate Assessment of Academic Proficiency
Education Assessment Series
The New Jersey College Basic Skills Placement Test

PORTFOLIO ASSESSMENTS OF WRITING SKILLS

Nancy Baker Blattner
Director of Assessment
Writing Center, MS 4600
Southeast Missouri State University
Cape Girardeau, MO 63701
ph. (573) 651-2573
fax (573) 986-6198
e-mail: *c817wrt@semovm.semo.edu*

Donald Daiker
Professor of English
Miami University
Oxford, OH 45056
ph. (513) 529-7110
e-mail: *daiker_donald@msmail.muohio.edu*

Maggie Madden
Maryland Writing Project
Towson State University
Hawkins Hall Room 301
Towson, MD 21252-7097
ph. (410) 830-3593
fax (410) 830-2733
http://midget.towson.edu/~bbass/mwp.html

Judy Arzt
Director of Academic Resources Center
Saint Joseph College
West Hartford, CT 06117
ph. (860) 232-4571, ext. 514
fax (860) 231-8396

Pat Belanoff
Director, Writing Program
The State University at Stony Brook
Department of English
Stony Brook, NY 11794
ph. (516) 632-7390
fax (516) 632-7121
e-mail: *pbelanoff@ccmail.sunysb.edu*

Marge Tebo-Messina
Winthrop University
210 Tillman Hall
Rock Hill, SC 29733
ph. (803) 323-2341
fax (803) 323-2359
e-mail: *tebomessinam@winthrop.edu*

Brian Huot
University of Louisville
Department of English
Louisville, KY 40292-0001
ph. (502) 852-6896
fax (502) 852-4182

LOCALLY-DEVELOPED WRITING ASSESSMENT

Spalding University (Writing skills assessed at end of 64 hours)
M. Janice Murphy
Provost and Dean of Graduate Studies
851 South Fourth Street
Louisville, Kentucky 40203
ph. (502) 585-7101
fax (5020 585-7158

Lakeland College (Basic Skills writing sample upon entry and a series of writing samples used for general education outcomes)
Karl Elder
Department of English
P.O. Box 359
Sheboygan, WI 53082-0359
ph. (414) 565-1276
fax (414) 565-1206

Northland College (Basic Skills)
David Fuller, Academic Affairs
1411 Ellis Ave.
Ashland, WI 54806
ph. (715) 682-1226
fax (715) 682-1819

Shawnee State University (Basic Skills)
Dave Todt
Assessment Coordinator
Shawnee State University
Portsmouth, OH 45662
ph. (614) 355-2239
fax (614) 355-2546
e-mail: *dtodt@shawnee.edu*

Marian College (Basic Skills)
Constance Wesner
3200 Cold Spring Road
Indianapolis, IN 46222
ph. (317) 955-6016
fax (317) 955-6448

**Allentown College
(Basic Skills: writing samples from all incoming students)**
Dr. Karen Walton
VP for Academic Affairs
Allentown College
2755 Station Avenue
Center Valley, PA 18034
ph. (610) 282-1100, ext. 1342
fax (610) 282-2850

Internet Resources

The amount of material and potential sources of information about assessment on the World Wide Web are immense. Because the Internet is changing and expanding daily, addresses change regularly. If sites are moved, the old site will often include a link to the new location. The most accurate information available at the time of publication is included for each site.

This section was compiled and written with the help of Jane Lambert, research associate, Office of Planning and Institutional Improvement, IUPUI, and Mark Connolly, project manager for the College Student Experiences Questionnaire Research and Distribution Program at Indiana University, Bloomington. For additional information, please see "Assessment's Greatest 'Hits': Using the WWW to Enhance Assessment Efforts" in *Assessment Update,* Volume 9, #2, for an article written by Connolly and Lambert. Tracy Tyree, AAHE Assessment Forum doctoral intern, located and explored the student affairs assessment web sites.

GENERAL INFORMATION

Search Engines

For general sites about assessment, familiarity with search engines such as Yahoo, *http://www.yahoo.com,* and Alta Vista, *http://www.altavista.digital.com,* can make searching for specific information much easier. Some common search engines include pointers to education resources and sometimes to higher education specifically.

ERIC Resources

Searching the Educational Resources Information Center (ERIC) databases using keywords can yield helpful information. The ERIC Clearinghouse on Higher Education site is *http://www.gwu.edu/~eriche.* For assessment and evaluation, try the ERIC Clearinghouse on Assessment and Evaluation site *http://ericae2.educ.cua.edu/main.htm.* This site includes a subject matter directory on assessment, and databases of over 10,000 test descriptions, full text resources, and journal article abstracts. In addition, contact the ERIC Clearinghouse on Community Colleges via *http://www.gse.ucla.edu/ERIC/eric.html.* AskERIC, at Syracuse University, is also a user-friendly searchable site: *http://ericir.syr.edu.*

American Universities

For assessment materials from a specific university or college, the following site is helpful, *http://www.clas.ufl.edu/CLAS/american-universities.html.* From this alphabetical listing, you can link to any college or university in the US or Canada. This site also includes links to web sites of Canadian universities, community colleges, and international universities.

Internet Resources

The site *http://apollo.gmu.edu/~jmilam/air95.html,* maintained by John Milam, includes links to 121 institutional research offices, 119 higher education associations, 42 state higher education executive offices, 100 student affairs offices, 11 assessment offices, and 38 higher education research centers and programs. In addition, it offers articles and discussions about using the Internet for assessment and institutional research.

SELECTED INSTITUTIONAL WWW SITES

http://Biology.uoregon.edu/ Biology_WWW/Workshop_Biol/wb.html

"Workshop Biology" is a FIPSE- and NSF-funded project in nonmajor's biology education. Its Curriculum Handbook includes a model for assessing innovation in college biology education. The Assessment and Course Improvement section of the handbook includes a description of the action-research-oriented approach to assessment, the principles underlying the approach, results of a longitudinal comparison of inquiry-based and traditional teaching approaches, and data collection tools. The complete Handbook is available at this site.

http://ultibase.rmit.edu.au/

This Australian site is a clearinghouse of information sponsored by "ultiBASE: University Learning and Teaching in Business Art Society and Education." UltiBASE promotes the improvement of tertiary (postsecondary) teaching and learning. Sections at the ultiBASE site include resources; events; articles and reviews of articles; links to sites in Australia, the United Kingdom, and the United States; and "Choice Clicks" submitted by practitioners who use the web in teaching and research.

http://www.alverno.edu

An extensive web site can be found at Alverno College, recognized as one of the leading institutions in student outcome assessment. In addition to "Quick Facts for Educators," through the "Alverno for Educators" link users can read a publication catalog and find information about seminars and workshops at Alverno.

http://www.colorado.edu/outcomes

Ephraim Schechter, University of Colorado at Boulder, has created an Undergraduate Outcomes Assessment page. In addition to an extensive list of links to other higher education assessment resources on the net, the site includes "what we've learned" pages about assessment, student learning and satisfaction, and other assessment activities.

http://www.enmu.edu/~testaa

The Eastern New Mexico University Assessment Resource Office (Alec Testa, director) maintains a site with links to their assessment newsletter, assessment plans of both academic and support units, and information about the New Mexico Higher Education Assessment group and conference.

http://www.montana.edu/~aircj/assess/

This site, maintained by Cel Johnson at Montana State University, includes assessment plans collected from across campus, assessment techniques and activities, a bibliography, and links to other sites.

DISCUSSION LISTS/LISTSERVS

Discussion lists—also known as listservs—facilitate open discussion for anyone with access to the Internet. Subscribers can often access archives of listserv discussions. Useful are listservs offered by the Association for Institutional Research (AIR), the Association for the Study of Higher Education (ASHE), the American Evaluation Association (AEA), and the divisions of the American Educational Research Association (AERA).

ASSESS-L

Discussion on assessment issues (both student learning outcomes and student affairs).

List address: *listserv@lsv.uky.edu*
To subscribe: send the following one-line message to the above address: *subscribe assess <your first name > <your last name>*

CA-CR

Focuses on classroom assessment and classroom research, specifically the K. Patricia Cross/Thomas Angelo model.

List address: *listserv@nmsu.edu*
To subscribe: send the following one-line message to the above address: *sub ca-cr <your first name> <your last name>*

North Carolina Assessment Network

This moderated listserv provides an opportunity for broad-based and participatory involvement in both useful and critical discussions of what is happening in North Carolina institutions regarding assessment, both inside and outside the classroom. If you have questions about the list, send e-mail to the list owner at *owner-ncassessnet@ncccs.cc.nc.us.*

List address: *majordomo@ncccs.cc.nc.us*
To subscribe: send the following one-line message to the above address: *subscribe ncassessnet*

INFORMATION SITES

For more information on most of the associations and research centers listed here, see the Associations and Organizations section of this book (p. 63).

Accrediting Associations

National
Council for Higher Education Accreditation (CHEA)
http://www.chea.org

Regional
Middle States Association of Schools and Colleges
http://www.webness.net/msa/

New England Association of Schools and Colleges
http://www.neasc.org

North Central Association of Schools and Colleges
http://www.ncacihe.org

Western Association of Schools and Colleges
http://www.wascweb.org

Governmental Sites

For governmental sources of information and/or publications, the following web sites may prove helpful. Two sites with links to State Higher Education Executive Offices and to State Higher Education agencies are *http://apollo.gmu.edu/~jmilam/air95/sheeo.html* and *http://www.nea.org/he/abouthe/statehe.html.*

Department of Education
This site includes links to Fund for the Improvement of Postsecondary Education (FIPSE) and National Center for Education Statistics (NCES) and a Federal Government Internet Educational Resources page.
http://www.ed.gov

Index
The Higher Education Research Meta-Index
This site includes links to federal and state level education associations and resources.
http://www.irp.panam.edu/more_html/utpa_erlist.html

Higher Education Associations

Higher education associations in this section frequently address assessment issues. For a more extensive list of associations and their direct links, see *http://apollo.gmu.edu/~jmilam/air95/assoc.html.*

Association of American Colleges & Universities (AAC&U)
http://www.aacu-edu.org

American Association for Higher Education (AAHE)
This site includes links to the Assessment Forum project and to AAHE publications.
http://www.aahe.org

American Educational Research Association (AERA)
http://www.aera.net

American Evaluation Association (AEA)
http://www.eval.org

Association for Institutional Research (AIR)
http://www.fsu.edu/~air/home.htm

Association for the Study of Higher Education (ASHE)
http://www.coe.missouri.edu/~ashe

Higher Education Research Centers

Center for Postsecondary Research and Planning
(home of the College Student Experiences Questionnaire– CSEQ)
http://www.indiana.edu/~cseq

Center for the Study of Higher Education at Penn State (CSHE at Penn State)
http://www.psu.edu/research/irp/cshe/index.html

Education Commission of the States (ECS)
http://www.ecs.org

Higher Education Research Institute, UCLA (contact for CIRP information)
http://www.gse.ucla.edu/heri/heri.html

National Center for Higher Education Management Systems (NCHEMS)
http://www.nchems.com

National Center for Postsecondary Teaching, Learning, and Assessment (NCTLA)
http://www.psu.edu/research/irp/chse/info/research/nc.html

Nonprofit Testing Companies

ACT, Inc.
http://www.act.org

Educational Testing Service (ETS)
http://www.ets.org

Student Affairs Associations

American College Personnel Association (ACPA)
http://www.acpa.nche.edu

National Association of Student Personnel Administrators (NASPA)
http://www.naspa.org

Selected Student Affairs WWW Sites

http://www-isu.indstate.edu/dragon/home.html
Student Affairs Research Tools Archives

Located in the Department of Counseling at Indiana State University, this Web site includes information on student affairs-related outcomes instruments, on-line access to surveys, assessment and evaluation tools, and other research and assessment resources.

http://www-isu.indstate.edu/dragon/ix-indx.html
ACPA Commission IX-Assessment for Student Development
Clearinghouse on Environmental and Student Development
Assessment Instruments

This database of assessment instruments ranges from brief descriptions and information to complete descriptions and reviews. Instruments are indexed by subject, title, and author, and encompass career-related issues, environmental assessment, learning styles, outcome assessments, retention measures, student development instruments, measures of values and more.

http://www.utexas.edu/student/research/
Student Affairs Research

The members of the Student Affairs Research team at the University of Texas at Austin share information on the use of surveys to collect information, the design of information systems to assess student progress, and the publication of reports to assist in the management of student services. This page is also linked to numerous Web sites useful to student affairs professionals doing research. Examples include national reports, assessment Web sites, sources of assessment instruments, and data presentation techniques.

Multimedia Resources

VIDEOTAPES

Accreditation on Trial: Who Needs It?
A PBS sponsored videoconference (April 1997)
For ordering information, contact Carol Swain,
cswain@pbs.org or the PBS Customer Support Center at
(800) 257-2578.

Using a courtroom format, this videoconference examines
the changing value of accreditation and credentialing. An
attorney who is an expert in higher education law questions a panel of experts who represent both higher
education and business organizations. The program also
highlights new ways to certify the worth of technology-
based instruction and distance learning.

Assessment 101: A Video Guide to Designing and Implementing an Assessment Program
Video and accompanying workbook developed by Michael
K. Smith and Jama L. Bradley.
For ordering information, contact Michael K. Smith,
michaelks@aol.com or call (800) 743-1574.

This video provides an overview of all the stages of
the assessment process, with examples drawn from
successful assessment programs. The workbook provides
detailed checklists for faculty and administrators on all
stages of the assessment process and includes complete
assessment plans.

Assessment To Improve Student Learning Development: A Shared Responsibility
Supported by the American Association of Higher Education,
the American College Personnel Association, and the National
Association for Student Personnel Administrators.
For ordering information, contact NASPA, 1875 Connecticut
Avenue, NW, Suite 418, Washington, DC 20009-5728, ph.
(202) 265-7500, fax (202) 797-1157, or see Web site at
http://www.naspa.org.

Moderated by Ted Marchese of AAHE, a panel of experts
(Pat Hutchings, Charles Schroeder, Jacqueline Woods, Pat
Cross, and Gary Hanson) discuss key issues around assessment on college campuses. There are five sections to the
video conference: The issue, the stakes; Trends and developments; Questions of method; Assessment that works; and
Getting started. Each section includes comments by the
panelists, questions from the audience, and questions from
viewers around country. This video approaches assessment
from an institutional perspective and is inclusive of issues
important for both academic and student affairs.

Conducting Meaningful Student Assessment at a Distance
Tape of an Interactive Teleconference (April 1997)
For ordering information, contact Dawn Smith,
dsmith@enm.maine.edu or see *http://www.enm.maine.edu.*

Faculty panelists from diverse disciplines with extensive
distance learning experience discuss philosophical issues
and learner-related and methodological aspects of assessing
students at a distance. Specific methods of assessment using
case examples are examined.

Critical Thinking and Assessment Video Series: Introduction to Assessment (V341), Critical Thinking Tests & The Improvement of Instruction (V342), Teaching Students to Assess Each Other's Work (V343).
For ordering information, contact The Center for Critical
Thinking, P.O. Box 7087, Cotati, CA 94931, ph. (707) 664-
2901, fax (707) 664-4101; e-mail: *cct@sonoma.edu;* or see
web site at *http://www.sonoma.edu/cthink/.*

This series of three videos features Richard Paul discussing
assessment and critical thinking and answering questions
asked by a studio audience. The first provides a general
introduction to assessment, the second discusses various
instruments commercially available to assess critical
thinking, and the third turns to teaching students how to
assess each other's work.

Teaching & Learning in the Computer Age Videoconference
National University Telecommunications Network (NUTN)
(March 1997)
For ordering information, contact Old Dominion University,
Rm #129 William Spong Hall, Norfolk, VA 23529,
ph. (800) 293-7679 or (757) 683-3012, fax
(757) 683-4515.

This interactive videoconference provides an overview of
national trends and cost-effective strategies for using technology to improve teaching and learning. Featuring Steve
Gilbert, Director of Technology Projects at AAHE, the program includes discussion of assessment issues related to
technology and learning.

AUDIOTAPES

The AAHE Assessment & Quality Conference offers for sale cassettes of featured speakers and sessions. The following compilation lists best-selling tapes from the 1994, 1995, and 1996 conferences in alphabetical order by title, with presenter information and abstract as presented in the conference program. In addition, some sessions at the 1997 AAHE National Conference on Higher Education and the 1997 Conference on Assessment & Quality that directly addressed technology and assessment issues are integrated into the alphabetical listing.

For an order form, contact Mobiltape Company, Inc., 24730 Avenue Tibbitts, Suite 170, Valencia, CA 91355, ph. (805) 295-0504, fax (805) 295-8474.

The 1997 Conference on Assessment & Quality tapes are available from Audio Recording Services. For an order form, call (410) 642-4220, or see *http://www.ars.service.com.*

Accreditation of Distance Learning: Is it Possible?

Distance learning is learning where distance is irrelevant. That is, students can learn from teachers not in proximity, in places not on campus, and by means that utilize a variety of modes of presentation. Accreditation, historically at least, has focused much of its definition and demonstration of quality on the learning environment – the facilities, the faculty, the resources, and campus culture. With distance learning, does accreditation thus become irrelevant, or at the least present a new challenge?

Larry Braskamp, CHEA; George Pruitt, Thomas Edison State College; Jack Allen, Southern Association of Colleges and Schools; and Jeffrey Livingston, Western Governors University. 97AAHE-56

Active Assessment: Taking Responsibility for Improving Student Learning *featured session*

The speaker maps new challenges in program and institutional assessment when faculty, administrators, and policy makers start with "what to teach and learn" instead of "what to test." The emphasis on educational goals and disciplinary standards makes assessment questions more focused: Are students achieving complex learning outcomes? compared to what performance standards? to the level expected by students, faculty, and various publics? Answering such questions means creating assessment that enables a learning community to make and act on responsible judgments about the quality of student learning outcomes across a curriculum. In such a community of judgement and action, what is good assessment? Wise judgment? Appropriate evidence? Who decides? How do diverse participants probe what "taking responsibility for improving student learning" means for students, faculty, departments, and institutions?

Marcia Mentkowski, Alverno College. 96CAHE-83

Assessment and Structured Interaction: Two Main Keys to Dealing with Diversity *featured session*

Use of faculty-structured, student-executed group learning and revision of assessment and evaluation practices to take better account of initial differences in background and time flexibility can substantially improve the academic success rates of underrepresented groups (and of students generally). Examples are used from traditionally "difficult" courses including calculus (where, for example, the success rate of both African Americans and rural whites has been increased from 40% to 94%) and physics (where learning by the entire class can be consistently doubled). The presenter discusses underlying principles and specific, practical methods for implementing these changes across the curriculum.

Craig E. Nelson, Indiana University, Bloomington. 96CAHE-102

Assessment and Student Learning: Using the MBTI in the Classroom and in Campus-Wide Improvement

The assessment of student learning style is one approach to ensuring student involvement in learning. The Myers-Briggs Type Indicator provides useful information for enhancing educational assessment activities both in the classroom and in the broader campus arena. This session focuses first on uses of the MBTI in freshman writing courses and in classroom testing, and second, on successful uses of the MBTI in assessing student populations, enrollment patterns, and the campus experience.

David H. Kalsbeek, Xavier University; Norman Betz, Central Missouri State University. 94CAHE-33

Assessment as Involvement: What It Is Supposed to Be All About *keynote*

The speaker addresses the reality that simply *having* student learning outcome information does not create change and improvement, as many early assessment advocates had hoped. He urges listeners to ponder how higher education can move toward completing the agenda laid out by the NIE report *Involvement in Learning,* including the role of continuous quality improvement in such efforts.

Peter T. Ewell, NCHEMS. 94CAHE-3

Assessment of General Education: Developing Patterns of Evidence

The concept of patterns of evidence is particularly helpful in the assessment of the fuzzy concepts associated with the evaluation of a general education program. This session focuses on the procedures, measures, and outcomes associated with a comprehensive two-year assessment of a general education program in which the patterns of evidence concept was applied. The procedures and measures are cost-effective and appropriate for use on many campuses.

Michael J. Reich, University of Wisconsin-River Falls. 96CAHE-62

Beyond the Head: Assessing the Full Range of College Outcomes *featured session*

Much of the work in assessment has focused on cognitive outcomes, ignoring the broader, whole-person concept embodied in most ideas about liberal education. Indeed, focusing on standardized, cognitive outcomes measures does little to improve scores on such measures, while it diminishes college impact on other noncognitive areas. This session provides a plea for broader visions of work in assessment, based on a reading of both the conceptual and research literature.

Alexander Astin, University of California, Los Angeles.
94CAHE-81

"But Is It Valid?" Issues in Performance Assessment

Disappointed with the narrowness of multiple-choice tests, educators from elementary and secondary to postsecondary levels are turning to performance assessment. But despite its intuitive appeal, establishing validity of assessment processes and student responses and products is complex and challenging. The panelists, experienced as campus practitioners, address such questions as: Who determines what learning outcomes should be measured or judged, and how should this be done?, How are criteria and levels of performance determined?, and How can validity be established for performance assessment?

Peter Facione, Santa Clara University; Marcia Mentkowski, Alverno College; Barbara Walvoord, University of Cincinnati; Trudy W. Banta, Indiana University Purdue University Indianapolis.
96CAHE-88

But You Can't Measure That!—Setting Collective Standards for Faculty Judgment *featured session*

"But you can't measure that" is one of the first concerns faculty express when confronted with the task of assessing college student learning comprehensively. They mean it's hard to measure important outcomes like the ability to think critically, perform a science experiment, or interact effectively in a group. Although these abilities ARE difficult to measure, faculty can productively set standards for judging these outcomes in performance. Panel members drawing on their experiences suggest how faculty can set collective standards for measuring or judging the quality of student performance on complex outcomes.

Trudy Banta, Indiana University Purdue University Indianapolis; Barbara Walvoord, University of Cincinnati; Peter A. Facione, Santa Clara University; Glen Rogers and Marcia Mentkowski, Alverno College.
95CAHE-72

Celebration of Academic Citizenship *plenary*

During 1994, AAHE's 25th year as an independent association serving the higher education community, a year-long series of activities was held on the theme "Celebrating Academic Citizenship." K. Patricia Cross, featured speaker, saluted the work of campus quality and assessment practitioners. She drew on her considerable contributions to higher education and the excellence of her own academic citizenship.

K. Patricia Cross, University of California, Berkeley.
94CAHE-152

Classroom Assessment and Classroom Research Across the Disciplines

Classroom assessment techniques (CATs) engage students and enhance their learning across four distinct disciplines-business management, literature and writing, biology, and political science. Presenters provide empirical evidence of the success and value of CATs derived from their individual and collective research efforts. Audience members participate in a CAT, and learn how CATs can be integrated with other interactive teaching techniques:—case studies, cooperative/collaborative learning structures, and group work—to achieve course outcomes.

Vicki L. Golich, Renee Curry, Regina Eisenbach, and Victoria Fabry, California State University-San Marcos.
96CAHE-72

Criteria-Based Assessment: Four Course-Embedded Instruments

This session demonstrates the use of specific criteria in assessing student learning in formative ways to improve pedagogy, curriculum, and courses. Each of four presenters offers at least one instrument that has been used successfully in a range of academic settings to measure student achievement in a particular course, program, or assignment. This session offers practical instruments and strategies immediately useful to the classroom instructor or institutions interested in course-embedded, data-based assessment of student learning.

Anna K. Carey, University of Cincinnati-Clermont College; William Craine, U.S. Air Force Academy; Barbara Walvoord, University of Cincinnati; Gisela Escoe, University of Cincinnati.
96CAHE-11

Embedding a Culture of Assessment Into Institutional Infrastructures *featured session*

All too often, institutions try to deal with assessment by making it an add-on to existing workloads—making it fit in to the institutional culture and infrastructure. When handled this way, it is hard to build and sustain faculty and administration support. This presentation explores practical ways to move from adding assessment on to building it into the core infrastructure of an institution, thus, moving it to the center of controversies about quality. Case examples and lessons are drawn from several dozen accrediting reviews of institutional assessment programs and from a research project evaluating the program review criteria of more than 25 institutions of all types. Specific questions are recommended that can fundamentally change quality conversations on a campus.

Ralph Wolff, Western Association of Schools and Colleges.
95CAHE-113

Empowering Learners, Empowering Educators—Lessons From Students' Ways of Knowing
featured session
Drawing on her studies of college student development, published as *Knowing and Reasoning in College,* and on her experiences as a faculty member, the presenter explores the integration of knowledge about the level of cognitive development of students in relation to teaching practices. The session provides conceptual as well as practical information for using assessment efforts to improve teacher effectiveness.

Marcia B. Baxter Magolda, Miami University.
94CAHE-82

Evidence and Action of Outcomes Assessment via the World Wide Web
Outcomes assessment practitioners at three universities share innovative uses of web pages and forms for outcomes assessment. This session highlights examples of preparing assessment plans, conducting and reporting course evaluations, implementing embedded course techniques, and conducting classroom assessment techniques. Also discussed are innovations at other universities including use of the web in portfolio assessment and use of other web technologies.

Alec Testa, Eastern New Mexico University; Ephraim Schechter, University of Colorado-Boulder; and Cel Johnson, Montana State University.
1997 Conference on Assessment & Quality-10

Facing the Future: The Quality of Faculty Work Life and the Restructuring of Faculty Roles
featured session
Universities are undergoing enormous pressures to change, reducing institutional expenses and student costs, focusing on student outcomes, and utilizing emerging electronic technologies. These pressures lead to restructuring administrative and faculty work and to the need to focus on stu-

dent learning and the quality of faculty work life in the process of restructuring. Implications for faculty roles are discussed.

Alan Guskin, Antioch College.
95CAHE-88

From K to 80—The Cycles of Learning
featured session
The presenter discusses the educational strategy of Motorola and Motorola University in partnering with global centers to meet the educational and training needs of the ever-enlarging population of learners. He also discusses the methods being used to improve the quality of education as well as reducing the cycle time of transferring learning.

Bill Wiggenhorn, Motorola University.
94CAHE-43

How Putting Students at the Center Changes Teaching and Learning: New Findings from the Harvard Assessment Seminars *featured session*
The first two reports of the Harvard Assessment Seminars were widely disseminated to the higher education community, and the results much discussed by faculty on many campuses. This session features the findings which were published in the third report from the Harvard Assessment Seminars.

Richard Light, Harvard University.
94CAHE-118

Improving Student Learning: Whose Responsibility Is It? *featured session*
Almost everyone wants to see improvement in student learning. Many agencies and organizations external to the campus—legislatures, state and federal departments of education, accrediting agencies, and the like—are assuming responsibility, through policy actions, to assure that students do meet higher expectations. Faculty and students, especially students, have been rather quiet in the frenzy to improve student learning. Whose responsibility is it?

K. Patricia Cross, University of California, Berkeley.
95CAHE-47

Indicators of Good Practice: An Assessment "Middle Ground" *featured session*
Building good outcome measures can be painful and time-consuming but is also not good enough. Without corresponding data about instructional experiences, we don't know what to fix. Research-based indicators of good practice, consistent with familiar guidelines like the Wingspread "Seven Principles," help fill the missing middle ground between what we know about students and what we can discover about their learning. Such measures also invoke the spirit of continuous improvement, while they remain true to the language and vision of classroom instructors. We need more of them.

Peter T. Ewell, NCHEMS.
96CAHE-4

Involvement in Learning: Looking Back, Moving Forward *featured session*

Four former members and staff from the NIE panel that wrote *Involvement in Learning* share their appraisals of its impact, the agendas left unfinished from the report, and their assessment of the needs of higher education in the 1990s.

Clifford Adelman, U.S. Department of Education; J. Herman Blake, Indiana University Purdue University Indianapolis; Barbara J. Hetrick, Hood College; Alexander Astin, University of California, Los Angeles.
94CAHE-119

Learning Organizations, Quality, and Higher Education *featured session*

What would be the effect of the quality of higher education if our colleges and universities were learning organizations? Why is it often difficult for colleges and universities to become learning organizations? What is a learning organization, and why would we want to be part of one? What difference would it make for us as educational leaders, for our colleagues and for our students, if we took seriously the concepts of organizational learning?

Judith Sorum Brown, Author and Consultant.
95CAHE-87

Linking Technology and Learning: Examples of What Is Working at Temple University and Indiana University Purdue University Indianapolis

Temple University and IUPUI are utilizing technology to expand community beyond the classroom and to transform the learning environment. This session will focus on the experiences of faculty and students in Temple University's Laptop Learning Community, a community designed to improve access to technology for commuter students, incorporate technology into the classroom, and increase students perceived levels of computer skills, usage and comfort. We will also focus on IUPUI's experience with its Joining the Scholarly Community course which uses instructional technology and instructional teams to link students to curricular and university resources. Objectives, outcomes, and future directions of both projects will be discussed..

Jodi Levine, Temple University; and Scott Evenbeck, Indiana University Purdue University Indianapolis.
1997 Assessment & Quality Conference-60

Making Involvement Matter: Lessons Learned About What Works *featured session*

While we know that involvement in learning matters, we know less about how to make involvement matter, especially in those settings where student involvement is difficult to achieve. This session explores the results of a national study of learning communities and collaborative learning in higher education and asks what lessons we've learned not only about how to make involvement matter but also about the role of assessment in promoting student involvement.

Vincent Tinto, Syracuse University.
96CAHE-85

Making Real the Scholarship of Teaching: Enabling, Assessing, and Rewarding Classroom Research *featured session*

Since the 1990 publication of Ernest Boyer's influential *Scholarship Reconsidered*, a growing number of colleges and universities have struggled to develop and support a scholarship of teaching to parallel the long-dominant scholarship of discovery embodied in traditional discipline-based research. Classroom research (CR), defined by K. Patricia Cross as "cascading intellectual inquiry by classroom teachers into the nature of teaching and learning," is among the most practical, promising approaches. This interactive session reviews the purposes of CR, provides several examples, and offers guidelines for promoting, supporting, assessing, and rewarding this type of teacher-directed, applied scholarship of teaching.

K. Patricia Cross and Mimi Harris Steadman, University of California, Berkeley; Thomas A. Angelo, AAHE.
96CAHE-24

Medicine Wheels and Organizing Wheels—A Tribal Perspective on Learning

This session explores lessons that can be learned from the world-view of indigenous peoples, which tends to be circular and highly contextual. This model is contrasted with work done in academic and business communities, which tends to be objective and polarized. From lived experiences in both worlds, the presenter incorporates both circular and linear approaches in experiential courses taught inside the collegiate environment.

KayLynn Sullivan TwoTrees, Miami University.
94CAHE-100

One Arm Around One Student's Shoulders *keynote*

The speech examines the changing characteristics of U.S. college students and the implications of those changes for assessment and quality efforts. He discusses recent findings about "what works"—the interventions that have been most successful in reaching the hardest-to-reach college students.

Arthur Levine, Columbia University.
96CAHE-3

Qualitative and Quantitative Assessment of the Extended Degree Program

In 1992, Washington State University (WSU) began offering the Extended Degree Program, an undergraduate degree completion program delivered entirely by distance education technologies. WSU has evaluated every major aspect of the program at the end of two and four years. Additionally, WSU is one of five Flashlight Project Coalition members working together to develop and test evaluation procedures to assess how electronic technologies are influencing teaching and learning. Presenters describe the methodologies involved and results obtained on student outcomes, program assessment, alumni, and perceptions of key constituencies.

Janet Ross Kendall and Gary Brown, Washington State University.
1997 Conference on Assessment & Quality-12

Realizing the Promise of Classroom Research: What Will It Take? *featured session*

Classroom Research is ongoing, systematic inquiry carried out by faculty to understand and improve their students' learning. It is a promising means for realizing the scholarship of teaching and CQI in classrooms. Realizing that promise is often a challenge. This session looks at successful Classroom Research efforts. Guidelines are offered to help faculty and academic administrators overcome common barriers.

Thomas A. Angelo, Boston College.
94CAHE-44

Regional Accreditation and Assessment: Challenges, Perspectives, and Lessons Learned

In this age of ever increasing accountability demands, accreditation has greater salience on the national public policy agenda. Institutions are more concerned about what is required of them and by whom. What do accreditors want? What are regional accreditation associations doing with regard to assessment? Do they have a shared vision of how institutions should address issues related to institutional effectiveness?

Sandra E. Elman, New England Association of Schools and Colleges; David Carter, Southern Association of Colleges and Schools; Steven D. Crow, North Central Association of Colleges and Schools; John Erickson, Middle States Commission on Higher Education; Larry Stevens, Northwest Association of Schools and Colleges; Ralph Wolff, Western Association of Schools and Colleges.
95CAHE-11

Self-Assessment: How Students Develop It to Direct Their Own Learning

An interactive team from Alverno—a faculty member, academic dean, research/evaluation staff member, and two students—explores results of 20 years of experiencing student development of self-assessment. They cover the developmental nature of self-assessment, criteria for effectiveness, strategies for developing it, samples of its performances, and evidence of its impact on learning in college and after graduation.

Georgine Loacker, Kathleen O'Brien, and William Rickards, Alverno College.
95CAHE-118

Student Tracking: Footprints Can Yield Valuable Assessment Information

"Use information you already have about students" is good advice for beginners in assessment. Tracking student progress, increasingly recognized by beginners and advanced practitioners as a valuable assessment method, uses existing institutional data. Experienced panelists give examples from two- and four-year institutions of the use of student tracking in program review and institutional improvement. Conceptual and political issues surrounding this methodology also are discussed.

Trudy W. Banta and Victor M. H. Borden, Indiana University Purdue University Indianapolis; Peter T. Ewell, NCHEMS; Jeffrey A. Seybert, Johnson County Community College.
94CAHE-17

Successful Uses of Teaching Portfolios

The teaching portfolio is an especially promising way for professors to assess and improve what they do in the classroom. Some institutions use the approach effectively, while others do not. This interactive session discusses important new lessons learned about what works and what doesn't, key strategies, tough decisions, and the latest research results.

Peter Seldin, Pace University.
95CAHE-105

Syllabi Analysis: What Are We Teaching and Telling Our Students?

This session includes a description and results of a unique two-stage project. Stage one was a systematic content analysis of class syllabi to ascertain the frequency and types of course assignments and examinations, grading criteria and expectations for student involvement, congruence between statements about and concrete illustrations of college mission and goals, especially in general education, and related questions. The second stage supplied feedback to faculty in participating departments to promote discussions about course objectives, teaching strategies, types of assignments, course rigor, and related topics. The project at a community college covered all classes taught in social science disciplines in fall 1995.

Trudy Bers, Diane Davis, and William Taylor, Oakton Community College.
96CAHE-51

Ten Years of Assessment at Harvard: What Has Changed? *featured session*

The speaker summarizes what has actually changed in undergraduate education as a result of ten years of Harvard Assessment Seminars. The themes of all projects are that they are student-centered, with an emphasis on helping all members of the university, both students and faculty, to do their jobs better. Light also lays out the two biggest challenges for the Harvard group as it works to strengthen students' learning experiences.

Richard J. Light, Harvard University.
96CAHE-44

The Assessment of Critical Thinking and Communication Skills: Linking Higher Education and the Workplace

This team presentation explores the emerging emphasis on improved critical thinking and communication skills to prepare college graduates for demands of the workplace. Particular emphasis is placed on skill-assessment research with employers related to National Education Goal 5.5., strategies and tools for use in professional judgment and decision making, classroom environments, and internship/cooperative education programs. Panelists consider particular applications and implications for accreditation, the health professions, human services, accounting, and improved postsecondary-business community partnerships.

Jo Ann Carter-Wells, California State University-Fullerton; Peter A. Facione, Santa Clara University; Elizabeth A. Jones, The Pennsylvania State University; Cindy L. Lynch, Reflective Judgment Associates.
95CAHE-75

The Capstone Course: A "Magic Wand" for Higher Education Assessment?

Conscientious higher educators trying to provide first-class major, graduate, or general education programs are often challenged by the need to integrate, update or fill-in-the-gaps in their students' programs of study. Similarly, conscientious assessors are challenged by problems in motivating students, involving faculty, or using more valid but difficult assessment options (like portfolios, interviews, essay exams, and performance appraisals). This session suggests that capstone courses can help solve all these problems and more, while upholding the highest standards of both pedagogy and measurement. Lessons learned from a major capstone course and other potential applications are detailed.

Reid Johnson and Betsy E. Brown, Winthrop University.
95CAHE-16

The Department as Fulcrum for Change
featured session

In *Policy Perspectives,* the Pew Higher Education Roundtable argued that the academic department holds the key to restructuring American colleges and universities. Departments, as faculty collectives, have the capacity to recast curricula, to shift the balance between teaching and research, and to bring a collective voice to discussions of academic change. The presenter uses the experience of the campus Roundtables—convened by the Pew Program—to focus on ways to make the tension between the need for academic reform and the disciplinary loyalties of departments and individual faculty a creative one. He also discusses what does and doesn't work in getting departments to take collective responsibility for their own restructuring.

Robert Zemsky, University of Pennsylvania.
95CAHE-49

The Leading Edge of Generation X: Time, Content, and Performance in Higher Education
featured session

This presentation features national time-series data from two cohorts: the "trailing edge of the baby-boomers" (high school class of 1972) and the "leading edge of Generation X" (high school class of 1982).

Clifford Adelman, U.S. Department of Education.
95CAHE-133

The Paradigm Shift Required *featured session*

To improve education requires a change in the fundamental paradigms of the teaching/learning process, with new roles for faculty and new responsibilities for students. When these transformations occur, management changes also are demanded. How to promote systems thinking in approaching higher education while simultaneously increasing the autonomy of the individual parts of the system is the central theme of this presentation.

Myron Tribus, Dartmouth University.
94CAHE-4

The Unexamined University: If the Public Only Knew . . . *featured session*

The institutional corollary to the Platonic admonition that "the unexamined life is not worth living" is that "the unexamined institution is not worth attending." This talk explores the irony that the one societal institution dedicated to critical reflection rarely turns its analytical skills on itself. A list of questions that most institutions ought to be able to answer—but cannot—is shared, along with suggested approaches for beginning to answer these questions and the implications such answers have for the work of the academy.

Karl Schilling, Miami University.
96CAHE-124

The Uses of Assessment

After a brief review of the development and components of a Comprehensive Assessment Program, a team of faculty members demonstrates how assessment has led to a variety of improvements institution-wide, including changes in the design of syllabi and guidelines for specific assignments, changes in curricula for both general education and major programs, and faculty development.

Jean P. O'Brien, Donald W. Farmer, Cheryl O'Hara, and Robert Paoletti, King's College.
95CAHE-35

Use of Assessment: The Connection Between Assessment and Quality

Many strategies enhance use of assessment data by campus decision-makers, from the Board of Governors to faculty, administrators, and staff. Use is the critical link between assessment for quality improvement and assessment for accountability. A president, vice president, faculty member, and student discuss successful strategies in enhancing use of assessment data.

Candace Young, W. Jack Magruder, and Lanny Morley, Northeast Missouri State University; Joseph J. Bambenek, Massachusetts Institute of Technology.
95CAHE-40

Using Electronic Portfolios/Resumes for Improving Education

Winona State University (WSU) developed an electronic resume/portfolio program that incorporates sound, video, music, pictures, and text to create a portfolio of the future. The format of the program emphasizes what students can do, rather than just grades. This presentation includes a discussion of the potential of this cutting edge technology.

Darrell Krueger, Susan Hatfield, and Dennis Pack, Winona State University.
1997 Conference on Assessment & Quality-27

Using Information on Psychological Type to Improve the Educational Experiences of Students
featured session

This session focuses on use of the Indicator as a research tool. It covers scores, type tables, and specific applications related to admissions, personal growth of students, academic advisement, choice of major, and learning styles. The model provides new insights for administrative decisions and teaching strategies. The session ends with two models: one for grouping students to enrich class understanding of the topic being studied, and the other for using student-consultants to help faculty fine-tune their teaching to all types of students.

Mary H. McCaulley, Center for the Applications of Psychological Type.
94CAHE-7

Using Multimedia to Improve Student Learning

In 1994, Xavier University of Louisiana's Center for the Advancement of Teaching developed an incentive program to support faculty across curricula to develop multimedia to use in electronic classrooms and computer labs. This program provided a highly structured transition from traditional teaching methods to new techniques that incorporate technology into classroom presentations and provide new opportunities for students to learn on their own outside of class. This presentation shares what was learned about the effects of technology on student learning through surveys, focus groups, and classroom research projects.

Elizabeth Barron, Susan Spillman, and Todd Stanislav, Xavier University of Louisiana.
97AAHE-42

Visions of Quality in Undergraduate Education for the 21st Century *featured session*

This session explores what students need to learn and how to ensure that they receive a quality education at the turn of the century. Emphasis is placed on devising creative strategies for assessing the quality of undergraduate education.

Beverly Guy-Sheftall, Spelman College.
95CAHE-89

Vital Statistics: Developing Appropriate State-Level Performance Indicators *featured session*

Heightened accountability concerns in hard times, as well as rising demands for consumer protection, have led a growing number of states to design or mandate performance indicator systems for their public colleges and universities. Increasingly, such indicators go beyond traditional input and efficiency measures to address instructional practices and/or student experiences. Increasingly, states are involving higher education's customers in their design. This session presents a national picture of these trends, punctuated by the lessons learned by one state in attempting to deploy such indicators.

Peter T. Ewell, NCHEMS; Margaret Miller, State Council for Higher Education for Virginia.
95CAHE-51

Whither Accreditation? *keynote*

Is there a need to strengthen accreditation to head off further federal and state regulations, or did the 1994 election signal an era of deregulation? Would strengthened regional accreditation be unnecessarily intrusive? Should there be common threshold standards across the nation, or should standards be left entirely to regional accrediting bodies? Should accreditation move from resource inputs towards student learning outcomes as a measure of quality? These questions are addressed by the president of the American Council on Education.

Robert Atwell, American Council on Education.
95CAHE-4

Technology

Technology and assessment need to be addressed in two ways: examining evidence about the impact of technology and examining the specific effects of educational technology on student outcomes. Although little substantive work has yet been published on either subject, the following examples of materials are illustrative.

In addition, sessions at the 1997 AAHE National Conference on Higher Education and the 1997 AAHE Conference on Assessment & Quality directly addressed technology and assessment issues. Abstracts are presented here and in the Audiotapes section. See the Multimedia Resources section for ordering information.

Readers can assist the editors in developing this technology section by submitting information about potential resources. Please call, write, e-mail, or fax your suggestions to the AAHE Assessment Forum.

GENERAL RESOURCES

AAHE Technology Projects Listserv

AAHESGIT is a moderated listserv on topics of teaching, learning, and information technology. Conversation on this listserv occasionally addresses assessment issues. With an e-mail account that allows sending and receiving messages on the Internet, anyone can participate in this ongoing discussion. To subscribe, leave the subject line blank and send the message *SUBSCRIBE AAHESGIT <your first name> <your last name>* to the Internet address *LISTPROC@LIST.CREN.NET.*

Case Studies in Evaluating the Benefits and Costs of Mediated Instruction/Distributed Learning.

Frank Jewett, Project Director
Information Resources and Technology
Chancellor's Office, California State University
P.O. Box 3842
Seal Beach, CA 90740-7842
ph. (562) 985-9156
e-mail: *frank_jewett@calstate.edu*
http://www.educom.edu/program/nlii/ meetings/orleans97/recRead.html

This two year project (1997-1999) will develop estimates of the benefits and costs associated with various types of distance education and distributed learning delivery methods in higher education. Based upon the cost data obtained, a simulation model that estimates the cost of expanding a campus using alternative technologies will be developed. Case studies from ten institutions will be developed to obtain data on the benefits and costs of specific distributed instructional delivery modes. Benefit assessments will be based primarily upon comparisons of the educational outcomes between similar courses delivered by different means.

Center for Teaching & Learning (CTL) at Washington State University

Gary Brown
Associate Director
The Center for Teaching & Learning
Washington State University
ITB 2008
PO Box 641223
Pullman, WA 99164-1223
ph. (509) 335-1352
fax (509) 335-1362

The Center for Teaching & Learning uses assessment as the linchpin in its efforts to integrate technology in ways to enhance learning. To assess various implementations of technology across the teaching and learning spectrum, the CTL employs a battery of instruments. As a formative tool, the CTL uses an online version of Angelo's and Cross's Teaching Goals Inventory combined with a companion Learning Goals inventory. Flashlight Project survey tools have been deployed widely and effectively (see below). The CTL complements these tools with a variety of additional instruments as well as controlled, field, and qualitative research methods. For more information, visit the WSU CTL web site at *http://www.ctl.wsu.edu/top_CTL-research/*

Flashlight Project

Stephen C. Ehrmann
AAHE
One Dupont Circle, Suite 360
Washington, DC 20036
ph. (202) 293-6440
fax (202) 293-0073
e-mail: *Sehrmann@aahe.org*
http://www.wiche.edu/flshlght/flash.htm

The Flashlight Project has been developing survey questions, cost analysis procedures, and other evaluative tools for educators with the goal of helping departments and institutions monitor how technology is helping and hindering efforts to improve education. The first element of the Flashlight Project, survey and interview questions for current students, was released in February 1997. For more information, contact Stephen C. Ehrmann, or see the Project Web page. To schedule Flashlight training and information sessions, contact Amanda Antico, program associate, at (202) 293-6440, ext. 38, or *antico@clark.net.*

McCollum, K. (1997, February 21). A Professor Divides His Class in Two to Test Value of On-Line Instruction. *Chronicle of Higher Education*, p. A23.
(See also the on-line article by same author *Academe Today: Of Note on the Net*, January 30, 1997. URL *http://chronicle.com)*
These articles describe a study conducted by Jerald G. Schutte, professor of sociology, California State University, Northridge in the fall of 1996. Schutte randomly divided his class into two groups: one group received traditional instruction and the other group was taught virtually on the World Wide Web. Schutte reports that "the virtual class scored an average of 20% higher than the traditional class." The on-line version of this article includes links to the web sites used by Schutte. For a description of the study, see *http://www.csun.edu/sociology/virexp.htm.* The students in the virtual course used the following web site: *http://www.csun.edu/~vcsoc00i/classes/s364v/toc1.htm.*

Moulton, J. (1996, September 3). *Curriculum Revision with Educational Technology: Improving Student Outcomes in Large Courses* **[WWW Document]. URL** *http://www.clas.pdx.edu/edtech*
This site describes a FIPSE-funded project being conducted at Portland State University: "The project attempts to improve students' experiences in a cost effective manner, establish an infrastructure that helps implement technology, and evaluate the effectiveness of educational technology on student learning. The project involves redesigning courses to incorporate technology." The site also includes links to presentations by project directors at various conferences.

Teaching & Learning in the Computer Age Videoconference
National University Telecommunications Network (NUTN) (March 1997)
Old Dominion University
Room #129 William Spong Hall
Norfolk, VA 23529
ph. (800) 293-7679
or (757) 683-3012
fax (757) 683-4515

This interactive videoconference provides an overview of national trends and provides cost-effective strategies for using technology to improve teaching and learning. Featuring Steve Gilbert, Director of Technology Projects at AAHE, the program includes discussion of assessment issues related to technology and learning.

Testa, A. (1997, March) *Using Assessment to Improve Instructional Technology: Using Instructional Technology to Improve Assessment* **[WWW Document]. URL** *http://www.enmu.edu/~testaa/aahe/overview.html*
In this workshop at the 1997 AAHE National Conference on Higher Education, Tom Angelo, University of Miami; Stephen C. Ehrmann, The Flashlight Project, and Steve Gilbert, Technology Projects, AAHE; and Alec Testa, Eastern New Mexico University explore ways in which common instructional technologies are used to enhance assessment of learning and, in parallel, consider ways in which assessment can be used to make instructional technologies more effective at promoting learning. This web site includes materials used in the workshop and links to other relevant sites.

Syverson, Margaret. *Online Learning Record* **[WWW document]. URL** *http://www.cwrl.utexas.edu/~syverson/olr*
The Online Learning Record is a "model of evaluation and assessment currently in use in the Computer Writing and Research Lab at the University of Texas at Austin. . . . The model integrates classroom evaluation, program-level assessment, teacher development, and research on teaching and learning." A session on this project was presented at the 1997 AAHE Conference on Assessment & Quality (see Audiovisual section for ordering information).

AUDIOTAPES

AAHE Conferences offer for sale cassettes of featured speakers and sessions. The following sessions directly related to assessment and technology from the 1997 National Conference (97AAHE) and the 1997 Assessment & Quality Conference. They are listed in alphabetical order by title, with presenter information and the abstract as presented in the conference program.

For an order form, contact Mobiltape Company, Inc., 24730 Avenue Tibbitts, Suite 170, Valencia, CA 91355, ph. (805) 295-0504, fax (805) 295-8474.

The 1997 Conference on Assessment & Quality tapes are available from Audio Recording Services. For an order form, call (410) 642-4220, or see *http://www.ars.service.com.*

Accreditation of Distance Learning: Is it Possible?
Distance learning is learning where distance is irrelevant. That is, students can learn from teachers not in proximity, in places not on campus, and by means that utilize a variety of modes of presentation. Accreditation, historically at least, has focused much of its definition and demonstration of quality on the learning environment—the facilities,

faculty, resources, and campus culture. With distance learning, does accreditation thus become irrelevant, or at the least present a new challenge?

Larry Braskamp, CHEA; George Pruitt, Thomas Edison State College; Jack Allen, Southen Association of Colleges and Schools; and Jeffrey Livingston, Western Governors University.
97NCHE-56

Evidence and Action of Outcomes Assessment via the World Wide Web

In this session outcomes assessment practitioners at three universities shared innovative uses of web pages and forms for outcome assessment. This session highlights examples of preparing assessment plans, conducting and reporting course evaluations, implementing embedded course techniques, and conducting classroom assessment techniques. In addition, innovations at other universities are discussed. These include using the Web in portfolio assessment and use of other web technologies.

Alec Testa, Eastern New Mexico University; Ephraim Schechter, University of Colorado-Boulder; and Cel Johnson, Montana State University.
1997 Conference on Assessment & Quality-10

Linking Technology and Learning: Examples of What Is Working at Temple University and Indiana University Purdue University Indianapolis

Temple University and IUPUI are utilizing technology to expand community beyond the classroom and to transform the learning environment. This session will focus on the experiences of faculty and students in Temple University's Laptop Learning Community, a community designed to improve access to technology for commuter students, incorporate technology into the classroom, and increase students perceived levels of computer skills, usage and comfort. We will also focus on IUPUI's experience with its Joining the Scholarly Community course which uses instructional technology and instructional teams to link students to curricular and university resources. Objectives, outcomes, and future directions of both projects will be discussed..

Jodi Levine, Temple University; and Scott Evenbeck, Indiana University Purdue University Indianapolis.
1997 Assessment & Quality Conference-60

Qualitative and Quantitative Assessment of the Extended Degree Program

In 1992, Washington State University (WSU) began offering the Extended Degree Program, an undergraduate degree completion program delivered entirely by distance education technologies. WSU has evaluated every major aspect of the program at the end of two and four years. Additionally, WSU is one of five Flashlight Project Coalition members working together to develop and test evaluation procedures to assess how electronic technolo-

gies are influencing teaching and learning. Presenters describe the methodologies involved and results obtained on student outcomes, program assessment, alumni, and perceptions of key constituencies.

Janet Ross Kendall and Gary Brown, Washington State University.
1997 Conference on Assessment & Quality-12

Using Electronic Portfolios/Resumes for Improving Education

Winona State University (WSU) developed an electronic resume/portfolio program that incorporates sound, video, music, pictures, and text to create a portfolio of the future. The format of the program emphasizes what students can do, rather than just grades. This presentation includes a discussion of the potential of this cutting edge technology.

Darrell Krueger, Susan Hatfield, and Dennis Pack, Winona State University.
1997 Conference on Assessment & Quality-27

Using Multimedia to Improve Student Learning

In 1994, Xavier University of Louisiana's Center for the Advancement of Teaching developed an incentive program to support faculty across curricula to develop multimedia to use in electronic classrooms and computer labs. This program provided a highly structured transition from traditional teaching methods to new techniques that incorporate technology into classroom presentations and provide new opportunities for students to learn on their own outside of class. This presentation shares what was learned about the effects of technology on student learning through surveys, focus groups, and classroom research projects.

Elizabeth Barron, Susan Spillman, and Todd Stanislav, Xavier University of Louisiana.
97AAHE-42

Glossary

The terms in this glossary are frequently used in assessment and in this book. Because definitions for these terms may vary, however, readers should be alert to specific contexts. Many of the following definitions are adapted from *Planning for Assessment: Mission Statements, Goals, and Objectives* by Lion F. Gardiner (1989). The quoted passages are cited by their page locations in this book.

Accountability
Responsibility for producing, reporting, interpreting, and justifying results (outcomes). External constituencies such as government or accrediting bodies often set standards of accountability for educational institutions.

Assessment
Production of information to determine the status of an activity in relation to the goals for that activity. Assessment includes gathering and analyzing evidence about how performance relates to goals and interpreting the evidence. Assessment results may be used to move closer to goals or to meet accountability expectations. (See Evaluation.)

Classroom assessment
Production of information to determine effectiveness of learning in courses. Classroom assessment presupposes establishing learning goals and includes gathering and analyzing evidence about how students and teacher are progressing toward the goals and interpreting the evidence, to maintain or modify learning and teaching strategies to enhance achievement of the goals.

Classroom research
"Ongoing and cumulative intellectual inquiry by classroom teachers into the nature of teaching and learning in their own classrooms." Classroom research is characterized by being "learner-centered, teacher-directed, context-specific, and continual." [See 30(78).]

Climate
The emotional tone or feeling evoked by an institution or unit, for example, inviting or hostile to new members, or nurturant or suppressive of innovation and change. An organization's climate reflects its culture and influences its capacity to produce desired outcomes. (See Culture.)

Continuous Quality Improvement (CQI)
A management philosophy that addresses the progress of an institution systemically and systematically to improve the quality of its processes and outcomes. CQI stresses a strong culture of assessment-based evidence for decision making in a cooperative, cross-functional way throughout the institution.

Culture
The basic assumptions and beliefs shared by an institution's or unit's staff and students about their organization and its environment. These assumptions and beliefs unconsciously affect and reveal themselves through the organization's values, behavior, and climate. (See Climate.)

Evaluation
Determination of the adequacy with which a goal has been achieved. Goals and their objectives provide the standards against which to make judgments. Information developed through assessment data is used as evidence in the evaluation process.

Formative assessment
Provision of timely feedback on quality to affirm or modify a process. Assessment evidence collected during an activity is used to improve its outcomes.

Goals
Statements of "what an institution desires to have (inputs), to be (processes), and to produce (outcomes) at a specific time in the future." [See 37(130).] Goals that contribute to improved organizational performance are characterized by specificity of language, high expectations, and knowledge of results through assessment. Broad goals have more specific objectives associated with them by which they are assessed. (See Objectives.)

Input assessment
Production of information about resources needed or present for achieving an institution's desired outcomes. Input assessment is used to identify necessary or available resources, identify use according to costs and benefits, determine feasibility of achieving outcomes according to resources available, and develop a plan for achieving outcomes with resources available or sought.

Inputs
An institution's human and physical resources. Inputs include students, faculty members, funds, campus climate, buildings, and an array of other resources.

Institutional research
Internal collection, analysis, and interpretation of data on the environment and/or performance of an institution, program, or unit.

Methodology
Activities or processes based on specific principles and assumptions involved in an inquiry procedure.

Mission statement
The assertion of an institution's or unit's fundamental aspirations. Mission statements generally describe an organization's purpose, role, and scope.

Needs assessment
A systematic study of institutional problems that interfere with achieving goals and that require solutions.

Objectives
Statements of aims or desired ends whose achievement can be assessed to demonstrate progress toward or achievement of their goals.

Outcomes
The consequences or results of processes. Outcomes are specified or defined by means of outcome goals and objectives. Institutions and units exist to produce specific outcomes.

Outcome assessment
Production of information concerning the degree to which an institution or unit has progressed toward or achieved its outcome goals and objectives.

Performance assessment
Assessment of ability that requires demonstration of the ability rather than response to proxy measures of the ability. An example is students' writing rather than responding to multiple-choice items about writing.

Process assessment
Production of information concerning how close actual processes are to desired processes.

Processes
Programs, services, and activities developed to produce desired outcomes.

Program evaluation
Determination of the adequacy of the program in fulfilling its mission, goals, and objectives.

Reliability
Capacity of an assessment method to produce consistent and repeatable results. A reliable assessment instrument or technique performs in a stable way over many uses at different times. Reliability is a precondition for validity.

Strategic planning
Long-term, often three-five year, planning at the level of the whole institution or unit that focuses specifically on adaptation to the organization's external environment and the future. Guided by a vision of the organization in the future, strategic planning attempts to position the organization favorably with respect to needed resources.

Summative evaluation
Judgment at the end of an activity of its effectiveness according to standards.

Systemic thinking
Consideration of all elements of an institution or unit and the ways in which these elements influence one another so that they are used and modified together to accomplish goals.

Validity
Capacity of an assessment method to assess or measure what it is claimed assess or measure. A valid assessment instrument or technique produces results that can lead to valid inferences.

Value-added assessment
Generation of information that enables comparison of intended and actual outcomes. Value-added assessment examines the differences between entrance-level and exit-level performance, for example, student abilities at admission and upon graduation.

Author Index

This index is comprised of authors and co-authors listed in the References section of the Assessment Library. For example, the entry for Rose M. Abler is 20(2) indicating page 20, reference number 2.

Keyword Index

This section indexes the entire Resource Guide according to the keywords listed here. The keywords are also listed on page 18 of the Assessment Library. The entries are both to specific annotated references and general page numbers. For example, one of the entries for "Assessment offices, campus" is 31(85) indicating page 31, reference number 85. The entry also indicates a reference to "Assessment offices, campus" on page 89. The keywords are listed here in alphabetical order; note that the symbols may not be in the same order.